CONFESSIONS ~~I~~ BLACKTHORN

PUBLICAN FRANK GILLESPIE'S JOURNEY FROM TYRELLSPASS TO BOSTON

Frank Gillespie

with

Paul Lennon

BLACKWATER PRESS

Editor
Ciara McNee

Design & Layout
Paula Byrne

Cover Design
Melanie Gradtke

ISBN
1-84131-669-5

© 2004 Paul Lennon and Frank Gillespie

Produced in Ireland by
Blackwater Press, c/o Folens Publishers
Hibernian Industrial Estate, Tallaght, Dublin 24

DEDICATION

To my late parents, Alice and the Colonel, my late sister and brother, Marian and James, and my children, Trevor and Donna. Love to you all.

CONTENTS

FOREWORD

FROM the first day I met him, Frank Gillespie has had a book in him waiting to be written. Wherever he goes, Frank is surrounded by people he knows and, more importantly, who know him. During the 1994 World Cup finals in the US, Frank was with Big Jack Charlton in Fitzers Bar in Fitzpatricks Manhattan Hotel in New York. There were quite a few famous heads around that night, including Eamonn Coghlan, the late Richard Harris, The Chieftains, Finbar Furey and Shane McGowan. There was a large contingent of Irish supporters present, too. Most of them were asking, 'Who are those guys hangin' out with Gillespie?', rather than, 'Who's the sham with all the celebs!'

Frank and I are not just great mates – we're almost related. For the last five and half years, he has been going out with my daughter, Melanie. Before I had ever met him, I had seen him on television in Australia demonstrating the making of an Irish stew with the confidence of a galloping gourmet. He was touring Down Under with The Fureys and stood in as a group member when one of the brothers couldn't make the early morning show. I wonder why?

The Blackthorn in South Boston is one of the bars Frank owns (although his business partner, Chris Barrett from the City of the Tribes, thinks he owns the other half!). It is one of the most popular bars on the east coast of America, and, as you will see when you read on, it has played host to many famous people including Big Jack, U2 and Albert Reynolds.

I have played many shows in the Blackthorn to packed audiences of young Irish immigrants. The atmosphere is always wonderful. That atmosphere will come across in this book, as Frank recalls stories from his boyhood in Tyrrellspass through to his experiences on the road to success; from humble beginnings to entrepreneur and, now, author.

Frank's not a bad singer, either. When, after a few pints, he launches into Joe Dolan's hits, he's a sight to behold, particularly when he holds the shoe to his ear and sings, 'A shoe, a shoe, a shoe, the only one I love…'. Frank's singing attracts an instant audience. When he and my daughter, Melanie, perform 'The Fairytale of New York', it's pure magic.

Frank is the only man I know who in his early days as a salesman managed to sell to a milking machine to a Westmeath farmer, even though he only had one cow. And he took the cow as a deposit! His ambition is to sell a double bed to the Pope.

I often visited Frank's late father, 'the Colonel'. He was a man you'd never see without a smile on his face. Even at 90 years of age, the Colonel was still able to sing the odd song and make us laugh with his wit. He was interviewed for this book only weeks before he passed away, but I'm sure he'll be reading the finished product from the best seat above.

Frank and myself have laughed together and we've cried together; that's why I know this book comes more from his heart than his mind. It's honest and sincere and, above all, entertaining.

Brendan Grace

October 2004

FOREWORD

IMET Frankie for the first time in Boston in 1986. It was one of
those moments when I immediately liked the company, one of
those meetings when I asked, 'Have we met before?' Of course we
hadn't, but I felt like I had known him all my life. Frankie then
invited my brothers Eddie, Paul, George and myself to his
favourite drinking well. That night led to an incredible friendship
with the band, the roadies, managers – so much so, that we re-
christened him Frankie Furey, or the Sham, the youngest member
of the Furey family.

As the years rolled by, I got to meet his very large and down-to-
earth family, from the oldest to the youngest, down in Tyrellspass.

Frankie has toured the world with the Furey Brothers and has
been with us at our happiest and saddest times. One of my greatest
memories of the Sham is when we were standing on the stage in
Carnegie Hall with the then Taoiseach, Albert Reynolds. Frankie's
voice echoed loud: 'I hope there's a good roof on this place 'cos
tonight it's going to be taken off.' The roar from the audience must
have been heard in Tyrellspass itself.

'Come on the Blackthorn!' my brothers and I responded. That
night, Manhattan was rocked into a frenzy with renditions of 'It's
a Long, Long Way from Clare to Here', 'Sweet 16'. Of course,
leading the choruses was none other than the Sham from
Tyrellspass – Frankie Gillespie himself.

Finbar Furey

October 2004

1

REALISING THE AMERICAN DREAM

JACK Charlton eased himself out of the settee, in the bottom floor of his suite in the Orlando North Hilton and Towers Hotel. He strolled over to the keg of Guinness in the corner of the room and pulled each of us a pint of the black stuff. As he waited for the heads to settle, Jack chuckled to himself as he always did when he was content. After depositing the pints of stout on the coffee table, Jack then ceremoniously lit up a fat cigar and pulled effortlessly to leave a hazy pall of smoke drifting upwards.

In three days' time, Ireland would be playing Italy in its opening group game in the 1994 World Cup finals in Giants Stadium outside New York. Throughout North America, Irish football fans were excitedly preparing for one of the biggest games in the country's history, but in that suburban hotel in Altamonte Springs, Orlando, it was an oasis of calm.

Just Big Jack and me. Me being Frank Gillespie from Tyrrellspass in the county of Westmeath, Ireland. As I sat there, I wondered how the winner of a World Cup medal with England in 1966 and myself had ended up sharing a quiet drink in the Ireland squad's base less than 72 hours before they would take on the mighty Italians.

Jack's status in sport is almost unique. He was part of Alf Ramsey's victorious English team of 1966 and was a key member of Don Revie's formidable Leeds United machine of the 1960s and 1970s. Jack was also a hero to Irish people the world over for leading the team to two World Cup finals and one European

Championship. Me? Well, I had left Ireland less than a decade earlier to escape the lengthening dole queues and the deepening economic crisis that gripped the country in the mid-1980s. When I arrived in Boston in 1985, I couldn't have rustled up the price of a pint in any of that great city's bars.

There was no denying that I felt proud of my achievements in the land of Uncle Sam: I co-owned the Blackthorn Bar in South Boston's West Broadway with Galwayman Chris Barrett. I still loved Tyrrellspass, Westmeath and Ireland, but America was the land of opportunity for me.

The bar trade gave me a comfortable living, but sport was one of my life's passions. It was my interest in these twin subjects – sport and drink – that sowed the seeds for this quiet pint in the company of Jack on the eve of such a momentous occasion.

***

I first met Jack when the Irish team played the US in Boston in June 1991. On the squad's arrival, I went up to Logan airport and handed out a stack of business cards to them. I invited Jack and the boys down to the Blackthorn for a drink, where I said they would be well looked after. There weren't many Irish pubs in Boston at the time, and to the players' – and my – dismay, they ended up in an American bar with an Irish theme that was situated down the road from the Blackthorn. Jack and the players couldn't understand how they had ended up there. They stayed there for about half an hour and then headed off.

A couple of nights later, this fella walked into the Blackthorn, and who was it but the bold Kevin Moran. Kevin quickly announced: 'Well, I promised you that I would come down for a pint.' Kevin had played for the Dublin Gaelic football team. A few of the lads who worked in the Blackthorn came from Meath, and there was great slagging over the Dubs and Meath.

Peter Farrell was one of the Blackthorn barmen at that time and being a proud Seneschalstown man – the parish that produced

Colm Coyle and Graham Geraghty – he wasn't afraid to take a good-natured pop at Kevin.

Kevin wanted to organise a round of golf for the next day, so, with my help, Tony Cascarino, John Sheridan and few others went off to the President's Golf Club in Quincy in Boston and really enjoyed themselves. Basically that was the start of the relationship between the Blackthorn and me and Jack and the Ireland football squad.

That was about the height of my contact with the Irish players that summer, because the squad was only in Boston for a couple of days as there was only one game organised. However, Kevin was generous enough to tell me if I ever wanted to come over for an international match in Dublin or take in a league game in England, then I only had to ring him up and tickets would be sorted out. That was an invitation I fully intended to take up, as football has always been close to my heart. While I had played Gaelic football at a competitive level back home in Tyrrellspass, I equally enjoyed organising soccer matches with my friends.

It seemed that my planned trips to Old Trafford, Anfield and Ewood Park would have to wait a while, because in early 1992 I toured in Australia as concert MC for the great traditional Irish group, the Fureys. But fate interceded when one night after a gig in Brisbane, the lads introduced me to Jack Charlton's son, John, who was involved in football coaching in the area. John and myself ended up going to a club, had a great night and struck up a good friendship. When I returned to Dublin, I planned to go to an Ireland game, so John gave me a letter to give to his father after the match. My first real chat with Big Jack was in the Pavilion Bar at Lansdowne Road, where the post-match functions were then held after internationals. Jack was delighted when I handed him the note.

***

At that stage, I still knew the players better than I knew Jack. So it was them rather than Jack who turned up at the Blackthorn in May and June 1992, when the squad was in Boston for the final leg of the Four Nations' US Cup '92. That's when all the so-called 'wild things' happened that are still spoken of today in the context of Roy Keane and Mick McCarthy's falling out in Saipan just prior to the 2002 World Cup finals!

During the first night in the bar, the lads elected me their social officer. The first thing I had to do was organise a stag party for Niall Quinn. I booked downstairs in Cuchulainns bar in the Boston suburb of Dorchester and organised for a couple of strippers to come down. But when we arrived in Cuchulainns, half of the Irish press corps was drinking at the bar. This made the lads nervous, so the strip show was cancelled. I had to pay one of the strippers to go home early before we had seen anything!

The question then arose as to where we would go. I said that there was no point in going back to the Blackthorn, as the place would already be jammed. But Packie Bonner piped up that we were definitely going back to my place − long line or not. It was mayhem in the Blackthorn, as the place heaved to the music being played by the DJ, Colm O'Brien − a first cousin of mine and the man who had been spinning the discs on the night of the horrendous Stardust fire tragedy in Dublin in February 1981.

The drinkers were cheering, asking for autographs, taking photographs and generally treating the lads as the heroes they were. Then the players decided to throw the bar staff out from behind the counter and began to serve the customers! For the next two hours Ray Houghton, John Aldridge, Kevin Moran, Tony Cascarino and the rest of them pulled pints and drew up measures of shorts. The punters were throwing money across the bar in a bid to get their attention. I think the bartenders did well from tips that night, but I'm not too sure how well I did. But the craic was good.

The one moment that summed the night up for me was when Colm played 'You'll Never Walk Alone'. The boys climbed up onto the bar or stood on stools and made the place sway.

Big Jack had accepted the Four Nations tour because it was an opportunity for the players to relax after six years of hard work. Jack was always chuffed when the team went out for a night, as it allowed them to get to know each other even better. I think we managed to gel them together that night!

***

The night of the final game of the tour was chaotic. While they were beating Portugal 2–0 in Foxboro Stadium, most of the players' bags were being rifled through in the hotel rooms. About $16,000 and a number of gold watches were stolen, and it took hours of negotiations between the hotel management, the FAI and the US Soccer Federation before the players were compensated. Poor Chris Morris had cashed his travellers' cheques for a family holiday in Florida, so he was mightily relieved that the players were not left out of pocket. Big Paul McGrath wasn't caught out, however, as he had hidden his money in his dirty laundry – the hallmark of a well-travelled man.

The robbery was a big downer for everybody, but by the following morning the incident was forgotten. The players got back to enjoying the final few hours of their east coast trip before most of them flew back to Dublin on Monday evening.

Kevin Moran had organised an outing to President's Golf Club in Quincy. Myself and Chris had arranged for three cars to ferry the 12 boys to the golf course. The players were to arrive at the Blackthorn by 10.30 that morning, with the tee-off booked for 11.15. They had orders to be back at the Park Plaza hotel in downtown Boston in time for the bus to leave for the airport at 5.30 pm. Myself and Chris were behind the bar at about 10.25, when Kevin walked in the door, with the rest of the players trooping in behind him like schoolboys in polo shirts, shorts and baseball caps. We asked whether they would like a drink before they headed off because they had a few minutes to spare and the course wasn't too far away.

'No, no. There'll be no drink until we finish the golf,' said Kevin. He agreed that they would call in for a few pints on the way back to the hotel. We went outside and began to organise who would go in which car. As Kevin opened the door to the car he was travelling in, he glanced up at the blazing sun. He turned to 'Razor' Houghton and said, 'It is very hot, isn't it?' When Razor agreed, Kevin decided that they should stay for one pint. He relayed the news to the players, who all agreed.

Aido McMenamin from Letterkenny was behind the bar that morning. 'What's wrong?' enquired Aido, as we trooped in for 'the one'. 'Nothing. We're just having a quick pint,' I said, as I took down the round which was simple. Twelve pints, which became 13 when I decided to have one myself.

Needless to say, that was the end of the golf. It might have been a Monday, but it turned out to be one of the greatest parties ever held in the Blackthorn! The music throbbed, the tricksters had a field day and the singsong beat all.

At any wind-down party, you always need to have eyes in the back of your head and this was no exception. I almost swallowed two golf balls which one of the boys – probably Aldo – had put in my pint glass! Quinny was doing his famous spoon trick, and I was the first person he set up! To those people who have yet to come across the spoon trick, let me unveil what is in store for you.

Two people put a spoon in their mouths and hold their heads down. They then take it in turns to hit each other on the head with the spoon. Unfortunately, when I stooped down I didn't know that somebody else was whacking the head off me, with a spoon held firmly in his hand! Quinny's partner in crime was David Kelly. As Kells took lumps out of my skull, I was wondering how the hell Quinny was laughing so much with a spoon in his mouth. When I looked up, there was David with a spoon – almost the size of a soup ladle – in his lámh.

In the middle of the afternoon, Quinny asked me to accompany him across the road to Deeney O'Malley's, where he wanted to buy a drink for a few old timers he had met earlier in the week. Unfortunately, by the time we headed back to the Blackthorn we were beginning to feel the effects of the 'golf day'. As we went in the front door, Quinny slipped and pushed me on to Colm's disco gear, causing about $300 worth of damage.

Mick McCarthy wasn't down in the bar but Roy Keane – who had enjoyed a late one with us the night before – arrived down at lunchtime. I was later told of the row between Mick and Roy that developed on the bus when the players finally returned to the Park Plaza. Some people have maintained that it occurred in the Blackthorn but that was impossible as Mick wasn't there.

As mid-afternoon drifted into late afternoon, many of the lads became hell-bent on staying another night in Boston. But I told Kevin that I would get into trouble if that happened. The phone soon began to hop, with anxious FAI officials at the other end in the Park Plaza. If I remember correctly, the first call came from FAI commercial manager Donie Butler, who told me to 'get those guys out of the bar' and that I should be ashamed that this was happening. I didn't care by that stage, because, in a way, I was hoping that they would stay on because the craic was so great.

I told the lads what was going on, and the reply I got from them was short and to the point: 'F*** Donie Butler, we'll stay for another pint.' Then the phone rang again, and this time it was Jack's assistant manager, Maurice Setters. He gave me a litany of abuse. Amid the jigs and the reels, we wound up the party and answered the SOS that had been sent out from the Park Plaza.

There was a heavy downpour when we went out to hail taxis, so we decided to drive ourselves. Unfortunately, my car wouldn't start! Eventually we got going, with a set of jump leads. The traffic was crazy due to the rain, but that didn't stop David Kelly from standing on the roof of Peter Farrell's car.

When we reached the hotel, the first person we met in the lobby was Jack, who grabbed Steve Staunton and marched him onto the bus. Ireland team physio Mick Byrne did the same with someone else. Mick had to pack the players' bags, and three weeks later the lads were still sorting out who owned what back in Ireland and England.

Just before the bus departed for the airport, Donie Butler came over to me and told me it was a shame what had gone on. I told him in no polite terms to 'get lost'. To Donie's credit, he wrote to me a few months later and thanked me for looking after the lads and said that there were no hard feelings.

With the players in such high spirits, the party continued on the plane home to Dublin with one hilarious moment. Aldo was squirting beer with a water pistol at one of his team-mates, but he hit Jack by mistake. Jack threw down the paper he was reading, turned around and told Kevin Moran that he'd never play for Ireland again! Kevin was dropped from the panel for a couple of games.

There was no doubt that the players appreciated the social dimension to that trip. When I went out with them in Dublin six months later, Denis Irwin told me that I wasn't to give any money to the drinks kitty, as I had looked after them so well in Boston. Kevin Sheedy was standing beside Denis when this happened. Kevin asked me how much Guinness had been drunk during that week in Boston. 'Five or six thousand dollars worth,' I said, to which Denis replied, 'Is that all?' I did well out of their visit as well; that week's takings in the Blackthorn broke all previous records.

***

That closed that chapter, until the next time I was back in Dublin and met Jack. The first words out of his mouth were: 'All I can say to you is that's some f***ing pub.' That summed up the way that Jack dealt with me and other people. He never held grudges. In fact, as time went on, Jack asked me to look after the lads when they were out for a drink in Dublin or elsewhere while on international duty. Mick Byrne would also have a word with me and ensure that I would have the lads back in the hotel by the agreed time. There was one occasion when we were down in Gibneys of Malahide; the curfew back in the Forte Posthouse Hotel, where the team was staying, was midnight. As usual, we were well looked after by Barry and Tony Gibney. As the clock ticked towards midnight, I had them all out except Roy Keane. When Roy and myself arrived back at the hotel, it was almost 12.15 am.

Maurice Setters was just inside the door of the bar, and he approached me as I walked across the lobby. 'Not good enough – 12 o'clock is 12 o'clock,' he fired at me. 'It's almost quarter past 12 and I'm holding you responsible, so I'll be telling the boss in the morning.' Needless to say, the next morning there was no problem with Jack.

***

So that was my introduction to Jack Charlton, Kevin Moran, Ray Houghton, Paul McGrath and Roy Keane and many others. What had started as a simple plan to hand out business cards at Boston airport in June 1991, had blossomed into friendships with a host of Ireland's greatest-ever sporting heroes. It had kicked off a chain of events that would see me become part of Big Jack's inner sanctum of confidantes.

As we sat in Jack's roomy suite in Orlando in June 1994, I raised a glass in honour of the team that he would guide to victory over the Italians a few days later. Yes, the journey from Tyrrellspass to Boston via Florida had taken me on a long, winding and interesting road.

2

GOING TO COVENTRY

MY mother, Alice O'Connor, was a Westmeath woman from a little townland called Meedin, which lies between Mullingar and Tyrrellspass. My father, Michael, was born in Stillorgan in Dublin, but moved around the country, as his father was a chauffeur for an English landlord. My father was six feet four, while my mother was four feet eleven. I obviously took after my mother! My father served in the British Army, and so was always known as 'the Colonel', a name he preferred.

We were a typical midlands household, with a mother and father who did everything for their children. In turn, the children strived to provide the best for their brothers and sisters. I'm the youngest of 12 children – a size of family unheard of now but common enough back then. I remember having a drink with a fellow in Boston one night, when we started to talk about our families. I told him that there were 12 of us, but his response put me in my place, because he was one of 19! He openly admitted that he didn't know some of his older brothers.

As is often the case when you are asked which member of the clan comes where, you need to put your thinking cap on. Starting from the eldest this is how the Gillespie family lined out: Kathleen (now Kathleen Spencer), Marcella (known as Massey and now Massey Goddard), Delores (known as Lolo and now Lolo Brennan), Eileen (now Eileen Silver), Michael, James (who sadly passed away in 2002), Claire (now Claire Dunne), John, Vincent, Eugene, Marion (Marion Stanway who sadly died in 1994) and myself.

I was spoiled by the older ones; indeed I was reared to a large degree by my older sisters, particularly when my mother spent some time in hospital. In age terms, Marion was the closest to me, being just two years older. We got up to all sorts of devilment and covered up for each other. I would mitch from school and encourage her to do the same so she wouldn't tell on me! Her death in 1994 hit me hard.

Like most Irish families in the 1950s and 1960s, we had precious little money to go around. What most Irish people lacked in pounds, shillings and pence, they more than made up for with great spirit and a sense of community that echoed that great phrase 'all for one and one for all'.

We lived in a small circle of houses in Tyrrellspass, known as the Buildings. Ours was a busy house, with so many of us living in it. It was also a great 'rambling' house, which is a term to describe a house where dances are held and music is heard. While my father played the mouth organ a little bit, my mother would organise the baking and make the tea.

My father had served in the British Army during World War II and lived in England for several spells. He was mainly based in a barracks down beside Chelsea's Stamford Bridge football ground in west London, where his love of football was nurtured. There were times when he might be at home and a telegram would arrive at the house in Tyrrellspass, telling him to report back to barracks. At one stage, he arrived back home to live, and he combined the few shillings he received from the dole with money earned doing odd jobs in the area. One day, I was helping him to bring in the hay for a farmer out near the bog, when we heard that the regional inspector for the Department of Social Welfare was snooping around. I never saw a man move so quickly across the bog, dragging me behind him, in order to reach the house before the inspector. We later heard that somebody had reported him for working while being on the dole. That was a disgraceful thing to do, as he had such a large family to support.

***

As things were tight, my father emigrated to England in 1959 and settled in Coventry, where several of the older members of the family soon joined him. In 1961, the rest of us left for Coventry. A few days before we left for England, there was a big auction at the house. All the furniture and any items my mother had were sold in order to get the few bob together so we could take the ferry from Dublin. People came from all around the village with tractors and trailers or donkeys and carts. It was a bit of an upheaval to leave Tyrrellspass, but it was also exciting. For a youngster like me, aged only five, it was a big adventure.

The first house we had in Coventry was No. 10 Canterbury Street, which was only a short distance from Highfield Road, Coventry City's football ground. There were always problems with the house, and the landlord was a bit of a tyrant. Like many houses of that era, there was only an outside toilet and we didn't enjoy the luxury of a bath. So every Saturday afternoon, my mother would march us up to the swimming pool where she paid for us to have a bath. That left us spick and span for Sunday mass.

There were a lot of Irish people in our area, with a strong concentration of Donegal families. Soon after we moved into No. 10, my mother began organising music sessions and inviting the neighbours around. I usually missed the 'rambling', because I was sent off to bed early, although I could still hear the music and voices downstairs. I didn't dare to open the door even an inch, because I would have got a clatter and been told to go back to bed. We eventually moved out of No. 10, when one of the older lad's bed came crashing through the sitting-room ceiling! We moved down the road to No. 61 and stayed there for a couple of years.

While we had little or no money, we were happy. My mother worked in a part-time job as a nurse's aid at Warwickshire Hospital. On Friday afternoons, she would pick me up from school and, with a few bob in her pocket, she would buy me a little toy.

Other treats included trips to the Gaumont cinema to watch pictures starring Cliff Richard and Norman Wisdom. Eileen and Lolo worked at the cinema selling ice cream during the shows.

I don't recall any problems with anti-Irishness, although I was pretty young to be aware of such matters. As far as I know, the Irish were highly thought of. In fact, the English girls loved to go out with an Irish fella.

My mother was always a great woman to write letters and she would spend hour upon hour at the table putting down the latest news. A birthday would never be missed, be it in the family or one of the neighbours back in Tyrrellspass. Our kitchen resembled a post office at times, with my mother sending off letters and then replies coming back.

My brother, Jim, worked at the famous Coventry Cathedral and actually shook Queen Elizabeth's hand when she had visited the place. There was a rumour going around that Jim fiddled so much from the entrance fee to the Cathedral that he was able to send our parents home on a plane for the first time! The other lads worked in the building trade, where there were thousands of Irish employed. In the 1960s, the reconstruction of Coventry was still ongoing after the terrible bombing the city had suffered during the war. There were still plenty of bombed-out sites in our area, and we would play in the derelict houses on our way home from school.

**

No matter how happy my mother was, I still think she missed home badly and, in particular, her own mother, Katie O'Connor, who lived in Meedin near Tyrrellspass. I suppose she just wanted to go home. Granny had put our name down with Westmeath County Council for one of the two new houses that were being built on the Mullingar Road in Tyrrellspass. In 1963, we got the house.

The first to come home were our mother, Marion and myself, with Vincent and Eugene following us over soon after. Mick, Jim, Massey and Eileen all stayed on in England. The lads stayed with our granny, while our mother, Marion and myself stayed with a great friend of our mother's, Mrs Gahan, who put us up in her small home a few miles outside Tyrrellspass. Mrs Gahan would always have a roaring fire on and the tilly lamp lit. She worked herding cattle for a local farmer, and I can still recall her with the sticks across her back in the morning. When we finally moved into our new house, we had to make do without electricity for a good while. So the tilly lamps were used.

Dinny Glennon – who owned a small garage in Rochfortbridge and was the local hackney driver – lived in the other new house. Dinny was the man we called on when we wanted to get into Mullingar, or to see the relations below in the Downs. He was part of the family, because wherever we went, Dinny went too. When my father came home from England with the few bob in his pocket, Dinny would be summoned to bring us into Mullingar. The Glennons still live in the same house, and one of Dinny's grandsons, Dennis Glennon, is now a regular on the Westmeath senior football team.

Across the road from us were Tom and Nancy Ryan. They had the first television set on the road. In the evening, people would gather around the telly in their house – there would be 20 or 30 of us in the front room – to watch *Tolka Row*, RTÉ's first-ever soap opera.

It was here that we heard that US President John F. Kennedy had been shot dead in Dallas in November, 1963. My mother came to the Ryan's front door in tears, to tell us that she had just heard the news on the radio at home. Kennedy's assassination stunned everybody in the area; the locals stood around outside front doors, crying and discussing the tragic event.

***

Ms Kellighan was the schoolteacher in charge of the younger classes in Tyrrellspass NS, and I made my First Communion under her guidance. We were practising for the big day for months on end. We were nervous about the priest coming in to examine us on what we knew, because it had been drummed into us that if we were not able to answer his questions, we would not be allowed to receive the sacrament. That would have been a major embarrassment for the family, especially with the suit already bought for the occasion.

When Father O'Reilly arrived into the classroom, we were still nervous, even though we had been learning every last line of the Catechism for months. 'I suppose you know who made the world,' said Father O'Reilly. 'We do,' we replied. 'God.' 'Good lads,' said the understanding Father O'Reilly. 'We'll see you on Saturday for your First Holy Communion.'

A few days earlier, we had made our First Confession, giving the usual list of sins that became second nature over the years: 'I didn't do what my mammy told me' and 'I said a few curses'. You'd get an 'Our Father' and 'Hail Mary' and you'd be quite happy. We'd come out of the confession box and compare the penance handed out. Anybody who got an extra 'Hail Mary' must have been really bad, while a decade of the 'Rosary' probably indicated that you were destined for the fires of hell!

Preparing for my Holy Communion was one of the few times that I fell out with Ms Kellighan. One day, she bundled us into her Morris Minor, six or seven at a time, and brought us up to the church. When we were there, she told us how to approach the altar rails. I forgot to put out my tongue to receive the host. For my sins, I received a slap across the face that I can still feel! Instead of going up to the church with my friends the next day, I was left behind with a bigger lad, Harry Rigney, who was hauled out of class to teach me how to receive Holy Communion. Once Harry was satisfied that I was able to hang my tongue out in the proper manner, he placed me on the bar of his bike and brought me up to the church.

It was the same ritual for Confirmation a few years later, with all sorts of threats being bandied about if you were not properly prepared.

***

In those times, people often lived in mortal fear of the schoolmasters because of the power they wielded. That was brought home to me when Marion and I were refused permission to return to Tyrrellspass National School after missing a short spell when my mother and the two of us visited England for a while. We were told that we would have to reapply at the start of the next term, so my mother got us into the school in Rochfortbridge, which was three miles away.

Instead of walking the short distance up to the village, we now had to get the 8.20 bus from the village every morning. In the evening, we had to walk the three miles home to Tyrrellspass, if we failed to get a lift. On some evenings, we would delay our journey so we could be picked up by some of the older lads, who were travelling home on their bikes from secondary school in Rochfortbridge.

When Marion and myself were accepted back into Tyrrellspass, it was time for me to go into second class and preparation for life a year later under Mr Jim Clarke, known by all as 'the Master'. Master Clarke was in charge of the boys from third class on and took no prisoners. Once you moved up into the Master's class, you sensed that you were moving closer to the big, bad world. The fun was over and he let you know it. So by the time that the new school year started in September, I was terrified going into the classroom. But after a few weeks, I settled into the routine. However, I still hated primary school.

My friends at this stage included my cousins Cecil and Dermot Dalton, who lived further up the Mullingar Road, Johnny Ryan from next door, Frank Glennon and Tommy Kelly of Gneevebawn.

It was during my time in primary school that I started to serve mass as an altar boy in the local church. I got on great with the priest, Father O'Farrell, who would often ask me to do the odd jobs around the place, such as sweeping up the leaves. Father O'Farrell had a few cattle, and when he needed them moved from one field to another, he'd come down to the school and pick me to do the job. Sometimes he'd ask me to bring a few of the strong lads with me, which didn't please Master Clarke too much. On top of earning a few bob, we were also missing out on school – perfect. Father 'O' was a generous soul; he'd give me a pound note for working on Saturday, which was a lot of money at that time.

But the real attraction of working for Father O'Farrell was being out and about rather than huddled over books in a classroom. So when Master Clarke told my mother that I spent too much time looking out the window daydreaming, he was right.

3

TEENAGE KICKS

Starting at St Joseph's Secondary School in Rochfortbridge in 1969, I knew I was set to take another important step on the road to adulthood. Going into first year didn't worry me in the least, as I knew many of the older lads from Tyrrellspass and they liked me. I also knew that I could match them at football, tackling any opponent no matter his size.

Finding myself in a mixed class of boys and girls was a Godsend! It was at St Joseph's that I met my first girlfriend, Ann Gilsenan, who was a year ahead of me and hailed from Rochfortbridge. One day, Sister Pious caught Ann and myself smooching in the cloakroom. I expected war to break out, but Sister Pious was into sports, liked me and was also very fond of Ann, so nothing more was said. Sister Pious later became famous for her friendship with Jack Charlton and her support for the Irish football team.

St Joseph's was a well-run school, and I enjoyed my time there. I was never tempted to mitch like I had done all too often in primary school. In fact, I often voluntarily went into school for the half day on Saturday. One of the teachers, Mr Sullivan, would sometimes collect me in his beat up Volkswagen, but maybe that was because he had half an eye for my older sister, Claire!

The teachers were very helpful and encouraged the pupils who showed any interest in learning. That even applied to the metalwork class, where Liam Corcoran and myself endured a baptism of fire on our first meeting. In my first class, my mind had drifted a long way from the finer points of metalwork, when a hammer flew just past my head. 'If you pay attention, Smiler, you and I might get along okay,' said Mr Corcoran. He never had to throw another hammer at me; from then on, we got on fine, as I developed a love of the subject that I have kept to this day.

I went on to get a B in metalwork in the Group Cert. For those of you too young to remember, the Group Cert was a state examination, mainly in practical subjects such as woodwork and metalwork. Students throughout the country sat it at the end of second year. Its main purpose was to assess fellas who were not too interested in going on to sit the Intermediate or Leaving Certificates, but who were ideally suited to becoming apprentices.

Like being taken on by Guinness in Dublin, getting a job as a fitter in Bord na Móna was regarded as a fantastic career option in the midlands. Being handy at metalwork, I sat the exam that the company set. Mr Corcoran had lots of confidence in me and gave me all the encouragement he could. But it was all to no avail, as I didn't get an apprenticeship. I can still clearly see the notes on top of the answer paper, which starkly pointed out that canvassing anybody in Bord na Móna or any local politicians in an attempt to secure a place would mean instant disqualification from the competition. What a load of rubbish! Dozens of highly suitable candidates found themselves unable to get one of the apprenticeships.

***

At the end of my fourth year at St Joseph's, I decided that it was time to move on from full-time education and to start earning some money. My first job was as a steel-cutter in Coyne's Engineering of Mullingar. It soon opened my eyes to the reality of working a five or six-day week. I worked on the steel-cutting machine for eight hours a day. The noise and sparks that flew off the machine were enough to drive any young fella demented.

I wasn't making too much headway in Coyne's, so I moved to Martin's Garage on the Longford Road in Mullingar, where I was to begin an apprenticeship as a panel beater. However, Peter Martin had other plans for me and he sent me up to his filling station at the other end of the town on the Dublin Road. You wouldn't see a car from one end of the day to the other, so I made it obvious that I wanted to get into the panel beating. That never materialised so there was no other option but to hand in my notice. That was a big disappointment to me, as two of my older friends, Liam Maher and Eamonn Whelehan, were employed at Martin's Garage, while the 'Young Boiler' Ryan worked down the road in Castle Motors.

From Mullingar, I made my way in the other direction to Tullamore, where I spent a few brief months working alongside my brother, Vincent, and brother-in-law, Seán Brennan, in Cappincur Joinery. Although the money was a little better, I could not see any future there.

***

My career prospects weren't exactly fantastic, but at least I had won the hand of Ann Gilsenan – though not without a few hairy moments as I did my best to see off her other boyfriend, Vinny Mooney. Vinny was older than me, had a few bob in his pocket and had a car. That said, I wasn't going to be chased away.

One night, I walked Ann home and was enjoying a kiss and a cuddle in the hallway of her house, while my friend Frank Glennon was waiting outside on his motorbike. Just as I was waving goodnight to Ann, along came the bold Vinny, who immediately spotted me.

'Quick,' I said to Frank, 'get the bike started now.' It was now that the full limitations of Frank's wheels became apparent. Bought for a few bob, his bike had just two gears and made more noise that a space shuttle in full orbit. Frank pushed the bike along the road in a bid to kick-start it, with me running behind him. We jumped on, but it seemed that Vinny was going to catch us up. Thankfully, the engine finally spluttered into life and we got away, leaving Vinny doubled in two with breathlessness. There's no doubt that he would have given me a fair beating. I chose not to stand close to Vinny Mooney in the months that followed.

***

In 1973, I began looking across the Irish Sea for a way to make enough money for Ann and myself to plan a future together. Thankfully, I was able to call upon my older brothers and sisters who had remained in England after my mother and the younger members of the clan returned to Ireland in 1963. My sister, Massey, and brother-in-law, Stan Goddard, came to my rescue by offering me a place to stay and a job.

Massey and Stan were living in London. Stan worked as an electrician and made me his apprentice. When I received my first pay cheque, I knew I had made the right decision. It was a cool £60 sterling. The biggest job I worked on with Stan at the time was installing lights along the side of the M1 motorway. That job offered me an insight into the lives of many of the Irishmen who had emigrated to Britain in the 1950s and found the going tough. Dozens of them – men from Donegal to Cork and Clare to Down – would be seeking subs from the foreman on Monday morning, even though they had been paid a decent wage on Friday. Most or all of it had been drunk over the weekend. Many of them had never gone back home, even for a short holiday or break. I felt the least I could do was to buy them breakfast when I had a couple of quid in my pocket.

While working on that motorway, I often thought of what Master Clarke had told me in his classroom back in Tyrrellspass: 'You'll end up diggings holes with the blacks in England,' he would say. Well, I did end up working with some of them and managed to learn more about life in their company than I did listening to him rabbit on for all those years.

Even with the money I was earning, Ireland was calling me home where my mother was anxious to see me settle. When my mother fell ill in 1975, I moved back to Tyrellspass.

***

My eye for an opportunity came to the fore in 1976, when construction of the GAF plant began on the site of the old Mullingar racecourse. GAF manufactured linoleum floor covering. After the announcement that a new factory was being built there, I monitored developments. When the first bulldozer moved in, I was straight in after it seeking a job with the construction firm, Mahon and McPhillips. My brass neck approach paid off, and I was given a job. The following week, I appeared alongside the bulldozer on the front page of the *Westmeath Examiner* with the headline proclaiming 'The New Replaces The Old'.

Mahon and McPhillips bought sand from Tom and Mick Ryan's sand lot, which was situated behind my house in Tyrrellspass. I assumed the role of overseer at the pit, and when the groundwork was complete I got a job as a driver with the firm before moving on to work as a security man on the site. Luckily, nobody wanted to steal anything from the place; because most nights my partner on duty, Tommy Rowland, and myself would drink our way through a bottle of vodka. Our bacon was saved more than once by the alarm clock ringing at 6.30 am.

From there, I moved on to the GAF factory floor, where I was employed on the colour line. It was dirty work cleaning ink trays with all sorts of chemicals splashing on to your clothes and the uncovered parts of your skin. The first fizz of excitement of working at GAF had quickly worn off and it was time for new horizons.

***

While Ireland was a country in a state of change during the 1970s, it remained a quiet, rural backwater compared to cosmopolitan New York, Paris or London. However, Hollywood came to County Westmeath in the summer of 1978, when it was chosen as one of the locations for the film *The First Great Train Robbery*. The story of a train robbery in England during the middle of the nineteenth century, the film was directed by Michael Crichton and starred Sean Connery, Donald Sutherland, Lesley-Anne Down and Wayne Sleep, who was better known as a ballet dancer.

There was a massive build up of excitement in the area when the movie circus set up base camp in the village of Castletowngeoghegan, which lies about eight miles from Tyrrellspass. Dozens of people from Tyrrellspass went down to take a gander at what was going on. I was standing there taking in all the excitement and watching the helicopters circle overhead, when this man – probably one of the assistant directors – asked me whether I knew any people in the area. He explained that he needed about 12 people to act as extras the next day. He admitted that he was fairly stuck.

I went back into Tyrrellspass, and gathered up a flock of people for the next day. My mother even decided to come along. We ended up working on the film for two weeks. I remember one man in particular, Jimmy Kelly, who was very nervous about his venture into the movies. I had to accompany him to the set every morning, but he'd still have to drop into Moss Fagan's in Tyrrellspass for the naggin of whiskey just to settle himself.

Our chief role in the film was as passengers on the train, which had been specially built to resemble a nineteenth-century engine and carriages. We'd be on the train going from Moate to Castletowngeoghan, and maybe back to Moate. While we were going up and down the track, the helicopter was whirring above us shooting film.

The excitement of filming increased when the stuntman, who was doubling for Sean Connery, had to jump off the train. We heard that Connery was worried about the speed that the train was rattling along at when he was scrambling along its roof. The train was supposed to travel at 35 miles per hour, but it was officially timed at 55 miles per hour. It's no wonder that 'James Bond' let the stuntman take over for the hairy moments!

Connery and his co-stars came in each day, surrounded by a great hullabaloo and with plenty of security. I only saw them from a distance. They came down in a limousine, did what they had to do and headed off. They weren't kept hanging around for five or six hours a day, unlike us extras. The only good thing about the waiting was that we were always sent down to the pub for a couple of pints. The problem then was that, when we returned to the set, the old carriages in the train didn't have any toilets. One day, I took Jimmy's hat and pretended that I was going to have to relieve myself into it!

The filming provided great amusement for all concerned and the few extra bob didn't go amiss either. Unfortunately, poor Jimmy Kelly, who could not have been even 50 years of age, died suddenly soon after. We cancelled the bus that was bringing us up to Dublin for the premiere. In fact, I didn't see the film for a good while after, but when I did I recognised many of the people involved and knew the areas filmed.

***

While Tyrrellspass was all abuzz during those few weeks, it soon returned to its quiet self, save for the ever-growing number of cars, lorries, vans and buses that trundled through it every day due to its location on the main Dublin–Galway road. Passers-through have often remarked on how pretty the village is, and that's probably down to the green that sits on the right-hand side as you head for the west. The hard work of the Tidy Town's committee brought Tyrrellspass to national attention in 1969, when the village won the overall award as Ireland's tidiest town. That was well deserved and I can recall the pride that the win instilled in the locals. The victory also brought extra tourists to Tyrrellspass.

As children, we learned all about the area's great history at school, including the Battle of Tyrrellspass in 1597. Oliver Egan's brilliant book, *Tyrrellspass – Past and Present*, gives a comprehensive record of the town from the earliest times, including a blow-by-blow account of how a Norman family, the Tyrrells, gave the settlement its name. Other books about the town are *Hello Tyrrellspass, Tyrrellspass Hello 2000, In Our Eyes* and *Richard Tyrrell*.

People who pass through the village may remark that it has not changed all that much over the years. That's a tribute to those who own the shops and houses. While there is a certain degree of development in the town, it has been achieved without spoiling the natural appeal of the place.

All Irish towns, cities and villages produce a raft of phrases and nicknames peculiar to their area. Tyrrellspass is no different and the nicknames pinned on fellas over the years are to be marvelled at. While I was christened Frank, I became known as 'Paddy' after my brother, Vincent, said, 'Here's Paddy home from England,' as I got off a bus in Tyrellspass Green. My brother Mick has always been referred to as 'the Doss'. Then there was 'the Frame', 'the Tit', 'the Mouse', 'Johnny Snot', 'Jimmy Buttons', 'the Half Hannon', 'the Pint' and 'the Half Pint' Buckleys, 'the Black' and 'the Terrier' Walsh. It seemed at times that nobody answered to their proper name in the village.

***

But despite the warm feeling of belonging to a 'real' community in Tyrrellspass, I could not banish the reality that local job prospects for people of my generation were bad. Like many lads before me, I joined the FCA, the Irish reserve defence force, partly out of a feeling of duty to my country, but also to earn the few bob that the weekly attendance and the annual camp offered you.

It was a nervous time for the country, with the Troubles in the North deepening by the day. The regular Irish soldiers from the midlands barracks in Longford and Mullingar were required for border duty, so FCA personnel were asked to take over their usual tasks. That was fine by me, because the money was quite good and I was able to give my mother an extra few pounds every week. After a crash course in full-time army training, we were handed our details, which included guarding the explosives factory at Enfield in County Meath.

We were based in Mullingar barracks full-time for several months, and were required to attend morning parade at 7 am. One bitterly cold winter's morning, I decided to leave the bottom part of my pyjamas on under my uniform to keep warm – a move that proved to be a disaster. Unfortunately for me, one of the pyjama legs was hanging out below my uniform, and the eagle-eyed Lieutenant Keogh spotted it. In the language of the army private, Keogh was a complete 'b*******'.

'What the f*** is this? Where the f*** do you think you are – Duffy's Circus?' yelled Keogh. 'This is the army and you're supposed to be a soldier, so why the hell are you wearing your pyjamas under your uniform? Get the f*** in and take them off you or I'll have you locked up,' bellowed Keogh. After reporting back on to the square for another inspection, I was allowed to join the rest of the platoon as we set off to keep the explosives out of the hands of the IRA.

The money may have been good, but the job was boring, as the factory was a dreary old place. I often walked around the place in the dead of night praying that nobody would attack – if they did, then I was not the soldier who was going to argue with them. They could have all the gelignite they wanted as long as they didn't shoot me. I was only there for the few bob. After a few months in Enfield, I no longer gave a damn about the north, south, east or west.

My duties offered me the ideal opportunity for revenge on Lieutenant Keogh. Late one night, he arrived in after a few pints. As an officer, Keogh was entitled to a meal at any time of the day or night, so he ordered a steak that the chef and I, as the duty soldier on call, had to prepare. I was raging that my sleep had been interrupted, but decided to make the most of this chance to put Keogh in his place. That steak hit the ceiling about five times and was then kicked the length of the kitchen, just to leave it nice and tender! I was delighted when the plate arrived back without a morsel left on it.

4

BOSTON BECKONS

FROM a young age, I had longed to live in America, but it wasn't until I was in my early twenties that I seriously considered following in the footsteps of millions of Irish men, women and children. My first taste of life in the United States of America came late in the summer of 1978, the year John Travolta and Olivia Newton John were stirring it up in *Grease*, Kerry were embarking on the first of their four-in-a-row All Ireland senior football title wins and the stop-start economic boom in Ireland was beginning to grind to a halt.

Brendan Lenehan, who hailed from the town of Rhode in County Offaly, was engaged to my sister-in-law Jackie. Brendan had headed off to Boston and become involved in a Gaelic football club called St Patrick's. St Pat's were looking for footballers, and Brendan rang me up back home and asked me if I was interested in going out to them for the summer. That handed me the perfect opportunity to leave for the States, although I was worried whether my job in GAF in Mullingar would still be there when I arrived back home.

I eventually plucked up the courage to approach the manager of GAF, Pat McLaughlin, to explain my situation. I could not have received a more positive response from him. He told me that he had gone over to the States at the age of 16 and that his first job had been sweeping the floors of a bank. He had returned to night school to further his education and ended up as one of the bank's managing directors. McLaughlin told me that there would be a job for me at GAF if, and when, I came back.

I was lucky to have Brendan to help me to settle in. As I subsequently learned from experience as a Boston bar owner, it's easy to arrive in New York, Chicago or Boston ill-equipped for life in a country which may be regarded as a second home for the Irish but can still be a cold, raw and uninviting place for the newly arrived immigrant.

In the months before I departed for Boston, I was experiencing back problems due to an injury I sustained playing football. So I decided to attend a bonesetter down in County Carlow, whose treatment consisted of asking me to put my hands against the wall and then pulling my leg back. He continued by applying an awful gooey poultice to my back. And that's how I travelled on the plane from Shannon and then spent the first two weeks in Boston – sitting in Brendan's apartment with this concoction pressed against my flesh.

As the money was running low, I decided to remove the poultice and start looking for a job. I received a phone call from the secretary of the St Pat's club, Chris Sullivan. 'You're to start working first thing in the morning with a fellow called Chris Barrett,' said Sullivan. 'Here's his number.' A quick call to Chris, who was a bricklayer, confirmed that he would pick me up at 6 am. True to his word, Chris was beeping on the horn of the van on the dot of six o'clock. I shovelled a few painkillers into me and jumped aboard, alongside a few other blokes, including John Higgins from Galway who was Chris's right-hand man at the time.

'Are you a f***ing student?' enquired Chris in a tone that suggested he was not seeking any disciples of philosophy or applied maths. I replied that I was a married man and then assured him that I could wheel cement. This seemed to dispel any misgivings he had about his new employee. I wheeled cement from seven that morning until seven that evening. My back held out fairly well, although I don't think it had much choice. 'You're not too bad,' was Chris' verdict as we drove home. 'You can come back again tomorrow.' That was my introduction to Chris, a meeting that was to prove so significant in shaping my life. I continued working for Chris for the next eight weeks, and we gradually became great friends.

During that summer, I even managed to get in a few games of junior football with St Pat's out in Brighton field.

When I returned to my job with GAF, I found it almost impossible to settle back in to life in Ireland. I went back to the States in the summer of 1979. This time, I quit GAF so I could spend three months on the other side of the Atlantic. At the end of the summer, I came back home to Tyrrellspass and jobs-wise things were noticeably quieter than before. I got a job as a sales rep for Halpins Tea and spent the best part of two years on the road, covering Offaly, parts of Longford, Kildare and Cavan and as far as Ballybay, County Monaghan.

After the success of the 1977 film *Smokey and the Bandit*, CB radio had become a big craze. Millions of people throughout the world had CBs installed in their cars, vans and trucks, and Ireland was no exception. Everybody had a code – or 'handle' as it was known – mine was 'Teabags in the Tyrrellspass 20'.

One thing I learned from my job at Halpins was that the old saying that Cavan people are tight is not true. They are the best of people, as I discovered as I made my regular delivery to the two shops in the small village of Billis, which lies not a million miles from Ballyjamesduff. In Prior's shop – where you could buy everything from a scythe to a sharpening stone, Wellington boots and every type of grocery – the dinner would be produced on the kitchen table for me. Then at the top end of the village, there was a shop run by a fella who bred Irish wolfhounds. When I arrived, he would close the shop and serve me up big, meaty sandwiches.

I enjoyed my time at Halpins, because I was meeting a wide variety of people and making a few bob. But selling tea was a tough old business, and Halpins were under fierce pressure from Lyons Tea, a much bigger company that had advertising behind it. When

I wheeled my trolley of Halpins tea into Quinnsworth in Naas, the fella from Lyons was emptying his van.

The yearning to get back to the States refused to go away, so in St Patrick's week in 1981, I decided to give it a shot. My son, Trevor, had been born on 20 August, 1980, so it was important that I secured lodgings quickly. My brother-in-law Seán Brennan put me in touch with the Bullman family in Randolph, a short drive outside Boston. A few weeks later, Ann and Trevor followed me over and we lived with the Bullmans. The Bullmans were a fantastic family who looked after us as if we were their own.

I went back to work with Chris Barrett. On my first day of work, I was not prepared for the weather. Heavy overnight snow had left Boston treacherous, but I reported for duty in my runners, when the least that was required were heavy boots. Chris had several jobs on the go at any one time. He maintained that we did the jobs that others wouldn't. However, without enough money to buy our own place in Boston, Ann and myself decided to return to Tyrrellspass at the end of 1981. But when I came back to Ireland and saw how bad things were, I immediately regretted that decision.

There was no use moping around when I had three people to support. One night at a function in Kinnegad, I bumped into John Mallen, whom I had worked for during the 1970s. John offered me a job as a rep for his new oil supply business, Mallen Oil. It began well as I clinched deals to supply oil to Goffs world-famous equestrian and exhibition centre in Kill, County Kildare, and Gallaghers Cigarettes in Dublin, amongst others.

My route took me from Tyrrellspass to and from Carbury in County Kildare every day. I would often meet the great Offaly footballer Stephen Darby out training on his bike. When I had the time, I would drive alongside and pace him for a few miles. I sometimes wondered whether I should have looked for a medal when Stephen and Offaly denied Kerry their bid for a historic five All Irelands in a row in September 1982! Stephen came on as a substitute on that famous day at Croke Park, when his brother Seamus, also a substitute, scored the last-gasp winning goal.

Selling oil was no problem. Getting paid for it was a different story, as Ireland slowly but surely became gripped by the economic downturn that would lead to massive emigration. I took my leave of the 'black gold' business, and opened up a snooker hall in Rochfortbridge, which I called Pot Black after the famous BBC programme. Unfortunately, the money I made from my own Pot Black was not enough to buy a loaf of bread, so I closed the front door and went on the dole.

This is not where I wanted to be, and I searched high and low for a job. To get me through, I worked for farmers out in the fields and painted houses. It was very hard going. Two incidents probably sum up that period. A great friend of mine at the time, Tommy O'Neill from Toar, priced the cost of painting a small council house in the area for just £15 – and that included supplying the paint! That would translate into a measly €19, but we could not turn down the work.

The people who owned the house were not poor but were renowned for not giving away a cup of tea or the extra potato. One day on the job, I was outside up a makeshift ladder, when Big Tom – or O'Nail as they called him in Tyrrellspass – shouted up to me that the tea was ready. Delighted at the word from below, I jumped from the ladder and went in to sit at the kitchen table. But there was no sign of the tea, nor of Tom, who I spotted outside doubled in two with the laughter. 'Is there something you want?' asked the woman of the house. 'A drink of water will do,' I replied and raced from the house with embarrassment. I was fit to kill Big Tom, whom I chased with a dripping paintbrush. When he finally caught his breath, Tom promised me an extra quid in my wage packet for the value he'd got from the prank.

Another day, Tom told me that a local farmer was looking for people to bring in bales of hay. We turned in hundreds of bales and received £15 each for the day's work. But payment was by cheque. I was supposed to play football with Tyrrellspass that evening, but I never made it. We went into the local hotel to get the cheque cashed, but had to wait for the manager to come back. We must have sunk about eight pints each on strength of the cheque and there was still no sign of the manager. So, we went up to the next pub – still with the cheque – and we had a few more pints there. Tom said to the barman, 'We're after trying everywhere in the whole village to get this cheque changed and no one will touch it.' Charlie Dillon, the pub owner, said: 'Well, I won't change it either.' We had a great night and still had the £30 cheque the next day!

That was one of the good days, but there were far too many bleak mornings, afternoons and evenings. By this stage, my beautiful daughter Donna had arrived into the world, so there was even greater pressure to bring in a decent week's wage. Thoughts of Boston and America continued to surface in my mind, now on a more regular basis. I would have preferred to stay in Ireland. However, three years had passed since we had returned home in late 1981, and the prospects of making a decent life for ourselves in Ireland appeared to have diminished rather than improved.

I finally made up my mind to go back to the States, thanks to the influence of my brother-in-law's brother, the late Willie Brennan, who ran his own small business making interior doors with his brother Seán on the New Road in Tyrrellspass. 'Paddy, go to America and don't come back for four or five years,' said Willie to me one day when we were having a chat. It was a piece of advice that I'm eternally happy I took.

Naturally, my mother was very disappointed when I informed her of my decision, especially as the kids were so small at the time. She asked Father O'Farrell to have a word with me to get me to stay. When Father O'Farrell asked me to hang on for another while, I replied, 'Father, I'm after doing a hundred interviews all over the country looking for work and it's getting very depressing. I have to go and do something with my life.'

It was even more depressing when Chris called me from Boston to tell me to get on a plane and come back over. I knew there was no end of work to be done. In truth, I was simply fed up looking out the window with no work in prospect. So in January 1985, I boarded an Aer Lingus flight for Boston. This time, there would be no looking back.

5

BUYING THE BLACKTHORN

WHEN I stepped on to the Aer Lingus flight bound for New York on 26 January, 1985, something told me that I would not be back in Tyrrellspass for a while. Ann and myself had got through Christmas with barely enough presents and festive cheer to keep Trevor, Donna and ourselves content. It was time for a change, and for me that meant returning to Boston, a city I knew and liked, and where I felt I would be able to make things happen for the four of us.

Before I left, I had arranged a job with Cunningham Electric, which was owned by an Irish-American called Tom Mitchell. Tom and his wife, Cathy, were very good to me and the job worked out really well. Getting up before sunrise to catch a 5.30 am bus to work didn't bother me in the slightest, for there was no end of work and Tom was happy to give me plenty of overtime. There were a few mornings when the freezing cold made me wish I was back home with Ann and the kids in my native Westmeath. However, I was determined to earn enough money to rent an apartment, so that they could join me.

By staying off the beer during the first few months of my renewed exile, I was able to save quite a bit of money, while also sending home hundreds of dollars. At this stage, I was also doing some part-time work with Chris Barrett. We even spent St Patrick's Day slaving away because we couldn't really afford to drink. 'We're working tomorrow, St Paddy's Day,' was all that Chris said to me the night before. In fact, St Paddy's Day was no different to most other days at that time. After work, it was straight home to the apartment to have dinner and watch a bit of television before getting ready for the next morning. Chris and I still enjoyed a few drinks, but the priority was to earn as much money as possible.

Like thousands of other Irishmen and women who had quit home to seek a job in America, we turned our hands to all sorts of tasks. During the winter months, there wasn't a lot of construction work going on, so Chris got jobs clearing snow. He had a contract for clearing snow from around the buildings of the New England Medical Centre. That was no easy task, as the buildings covered a couple of blocks. We'd often be there for two or three days, and then off for the same period. We'd be praying for snow, so we could make a few bob!

Brendan Lenehan and myself decided to rent a place together. By the middle of April, we possessed enough cash for a deposit on a small apartment. I'll never forget it – the walls were pink! But the two of us – with the help of my friend Brian Hickey – soon rectified that and within a few weeks the place was more than passable. Now, all we needed was some furniture. Friends donated a number of chairs and a mattress. We scoured the streets at night looking for household items that were being discarded for the bin men. We found a rug and a coffee table that was perfectly useable once a few nails and glue had been added in the right places. One evening, we even came across a fairly modern television set, and when I worked my magic with the oldest trick in the book – using a coat hanger as an aerial – we were able to pick up most of the main stations. We were over the moon as we stood proudly in our own home in America.

As we moved into May 1985, Brendan started working as a bartender in the Blarney Stone pub, while my job with Cunningham Electric was flying. Gradually, we managed to find furniture and beds for the two small rooms, and by the middle of the month all was in order for Ann and the kids to join me. I was so excited when the three of them arrived in Boston. The next day, I even brought four-year-old Trevor with me to work. We enjoyed a great summer in the city, even though the lack of a green card meant that the threat of expulsion from the US was always present.

We got a break when Joe McGlone – a proud Belfastman from Andersonstown – offered me a better-paid job with his firm, which specialised in the construction and demolition business. Joe doubled my wages to $90 a day, which was good money in those days. Without doubt, Joe's crew were the wildest bunch of blokes I ever worked with. Their dedication to their jobs was matched only by their willingness to drink. Joe also helped me out when I required a $1,000 deposit for a new apartment. Within three weeks, I had paid it all back. Joe said it was the quickest $1,000 that he was ever paid back.

I eventually set up my own construction company. I named the business Meath Construction, because I figured that Westmeath was too long. I ended up having a few lads working for me. Extensions, porches, painting and all types of jobs were the staple trade for Meath Construction. If there was a job that I couldn't do, I always got someone else to go in and give a price, so I'd make a few bob on commission. Thankfully, the business developed to a point where Ann and myself were able to get a mortgage to buy our own house. The day in 1988 when we walked through the front door of 25 Train Street, Dorchester, with Trevor and Donna was really, really special.

That summer, my mother flew out for Trevor's First Communion, and she thoroughly enjoyed her stay. There was a gang of lads working on the house at the time – Charlie Conroy, Stephen Darby and Gerry Hickey, who were all Offalymen; Mick Wright from the *Gaelic World* magazine; Patsy McDonagh and Connemara man Martin Grealish, who was also a boxing promoter. With my mother brewing up the tea and so many stories to be told, their 10 o'clock tea break often lasted well over an hour. But nobody cared because the craic at the table was great.

**

I secured a green card during an amnesty organised by the US government in 1988, which meant security for Ann, Trevor and Donna. I got the courage to go down to the immigration service office in Boston on the first day of the amnesty scheme, despite the dire warnings from other lads in the bar that I drank in at that time. They were convinced that it was a set up and that I would be arrested when I went down there. But I didn't care; I didn't want to live illegally any more. I turned out to be one of the first three Irish people who applied for it that day. Everybody else was too nervous to show their face.

I was absolutely amazed at how well I was treated. The official who dealt with my application shook my hand and thanked me for coming in. At the time, I worked with an organisation called Catholic Charities, which had a lawyer who gave out free advice. He did all the paperwork for me, and I eventually got the card. I put the word out for everybody to go in and eventually an awful lot of the men and women plucked up the courage. It brought in a whole new era for the Irish in the US.

It was also an exciting time to be Irish living in the US, as people were able to fulfil their potential. I know of fellas who had been struggling as plasterers in Ireland, but who got so much work when they came over to Boston that they'd have lads working for them. And when men got settled down with a home and a job, they, in turn, were able to bring out other relations and friends from back home. I brought out several people myself, including Ann's brother-in-law, Eamonn Dowdall, who lived with us for six months. Eamonn still lives in the States and has gone on to establish his own very successful painting and decorating firm.

**

Life was good. The fact that I was running a successful building business and that Ann and I had bought a house vindicated our decision to leave Ireland. However, our marriage was beginning to crumble. It soon became obvious that there was a problem between us. That reality hit me very, very hard, as it did Ann. I have never publicly discussed the breakdown and I don't intend to do so now. I prefer to look back on the good times we spent together and the fact that we were blessed with two beautiful children in Trevor and Donna.

I first met Ann Gilsenan when I was about 13 at St Joseph's Secondary School. Her family were originally from a little place called Dromone in County Meath. Her father, Hughie, worked for Bord na Móna. Ann was a year ahead of me in school. I suppose it was the night of the bonfire when the Gaelic football team won the under-14 cup in 1970 that we first began to see each other. The first night that I left her home after a disco in Rhode, I had my neighbour, Frank Glennon, to thank. I was down to my last few pence, so I borrowed two shillings off him to buy Ann a mineral at the bar.

We went out together all through our school years, and even my move to London to find work didn't come between us. Letters winged their way between Ireland and England, until Ann came over to work in London for a while. We had a very close relationship, and eventually tied the knot on 5 November, 1977, in Rochfortbridge. We honeymooned in the Canary Islands and lived in my parent's home in Tyrrellspass until we emigrated.

Trevor was born on 20 August, 1980 in Portiuncula Hospital in Ballinasloe, County Galway, and his sister, Donna, arrived into this world in the same delivery ward on 7 November, 1982 – two days that will be forever imprinted on my mind. Ann and myself are so proud of the two children. Through good times and bad, Ann and I stuck together as we tried to provide the best possible opportunities for the children. Our decisions to journey back and forth across the Atlantic were jointly taken. When Ann came over to Boston with Trevor and Donna in 1985, she worked extremely hard as a waitress in the Blarney Stone in Dorchester. Maybe it was the pressure of keeping things going on all fronts or maybe because we married young, but we weren't getting on. We separated in 1991, but promised that we would remain friends, because we had two great kids.

Breaking up was far from easy. There were a lot of tears, and it is not something I'd ever like to go through again. I did end up burying myself in the auld brandy for a while, and that gets you nowhere. Fortunately, I had great people around me. My best guidance counsellor was my business partner, Chris; at the other end of the phone was Finbar Furey.

Thankfully, Ann and myself have remained good friends, as I have with all her family. Any time they visit the States, they're always welcome in my house. I enjoy going for a pint with her father, Hughie, who is still a local character in Rochfortbridge. It was Hughie who helped to build the extension to my family's home in Tyrrellspass.

Ann has done a great job of bringing up the kids, and she's also doing very well herself in Boston. We got divorced in 1993. Over the years, we never had any problems over the children. Ann had the kids during the week and then I had them at the weekends. I took them to Ireland on several occasions, and Ann has also taken them away on trips. I suppose I was lucky that my working hours were flexible, as this allowed me to pick Trevor and Donna up from school and make sure they had their dinner before Ann would arrive home from work. In the mornings, I would often pick them up and bring them to school.

Trevor is now a carpenter and is into music in a big way. He plays lead guitar for a band called Roxie, who have played before American football games involving the New England Patriots, the 2004 Super Bowl winners. It's great to see him and the band doing so well. They have played all around New Jersey, New York and Connecticut. At one stage, I was pushing him towards a football career as he wasn't a bad player. When he was the Wimbledon manager, Joe Kinnear said he'd take him over for a trial. I hesitated, however, because I've seen too many youngsters devastated when they discovered the harsh reality of life as an apprentice footballer. London was also a long way away from Boston. Things have worked out well for Trevor, as he's now got a trade and is also playing away with the band.

Donna's doing great, as well. She works as a beautician, and also runs the Blackthorn for me at weekends. She takes no nonsense when she's in charge of the bar. I call her the social butterfly, and she says, 'Well I must have taken after my father'. It also makes me very proud to know that the children love Ireland as much as I do.

***

While building up Meath Construction, I remained in contact with Chris and we used to meet for a beer on a Friday evening. We even linked up for the occasional job. Chris would collect me some mornings, and we'd drive up through the Boston suburb of Quincy, where we'd see the people out mowing their lawns and watering the grass outside lovely houses. 'I'd love a house like that,' I often said to Chris. Today, I'm living in the area. And due to the large influx of Irish during the 1980s, Quincy has a big immigrant community, and four or five Irish bars.

While driving to and from jobs around the city, Chris and myself would sometimes chat about our desire to one day own a pub. It soon became our chief business ambition, and the opportunity arose in early 1990. Chris heard through the grapevine that a pub called the Car Stop was on the market. Situated on West Broadway in South Boston, the Car Stop was owned by a fellow from Roscommon by the name of Peter Kelly. Chris got me to phone Peter to check out the situation. I was well known around the area, and I didn't want Peter to know who I was, so I gave him a different name. Eventually he wanted to meet with me, so I explained that I didn't want to use my own name. Peter understood that I did not want our business to become public knowledge. He was looking for $545,000; on top of that, the bar required a lot of work.

Chris and I got on to the Bank of Ireland, which had recently opened a branch in Boston. We arranged a meeting with the manager Bernard Hayes – a lovely man from back home. He told us that he'd let us know in a few days whether he could give us the loan. Neither Chris nor myself slept too much that night, but thankfully the bank made a quick decision and we got the call the next day, saying that everything was okay.

We weren't buying the Car Stop on the turnover figures, but more on its potential. A lot of Irish people had moved into South Boston and there was room for an Irish pub. As I sometimes did in those days, I sought a bit of advice from the late Tommy McGann, who owned his own pub in Boston and would go out his way to help people. Tommy arrived down to look at the Car Stop, and told us that if it were his decision he'd buy the place. 'With your personalities and the fact that you are both fairly well known on the football scene, you should have no problem pulling in a crowd,' was Tommy's opinion.

So we went ahead and signed the deal. Between lawyers' fees and all the other additional costs, we had spent over $600,000. It was, and still is, an awful lot of money. With the bar now legally ours, we drove down to 'Southie' to open up. But the beer companies wouldn't deliver to us for two weeks, because they had to do a credit check. That left us in an awful predicament. We had no option but to buy the beer with cash, but we didn't have any money left!

I went over to see my good friend Brendan Lenehan, who had recently opened a pub called Cuchulainns down in Dorchester. 'Would you have any spare cash around? I need it to get the bar open,' I asked. 'I won't get a delivery unless I pay cash.' That evening, Brendan came up and handed me an envelope containing $10,000. I think we had paid him back in a month.

Now all we had to do was come up with a name for the pub and that was harder than we ever imagined. After spending hours and hours throwing names at each other and anybody else who would listen, we opted for the old 'Grand National' trick of sticking a pin into a piece of paper. Fifty names were written down on a list, and we closed our eyes. When Brendan and myself both stuck the pin into 'the Blackthorn', there was no argument. We were all delighted because of the historical link with Ireland through the blackthorn stick. For me, the name was really important, as I didn't want it to be called 'the Leaping Leprechaun' or something like that.

Chris and myself felt really proud of our achievement. I was thrilled that, little more than five years after leaving home, I was co-owner of a pub in Boston. However, the first few weeks were full of drama. Urgent work was required on the front of the bar, so we knocked down the whole front of the shop while remaining open for business. We had to take turns to stay in the pub at night.

The first opening of the Blackthorn took place on 21 August, 1990, but we had loads of opening nights. I suppose the official opening went ahead the following October, when the Fureys and Davy Arthur played a gig – even though there was no stage. That night, I stood on the counter to welcome all the customers and to thank the boys for playing. Just as I about to climb back down, Finbar Furey shouted at me: 'Get down, Frankie. I often seen a bigger head on a pint!'

Even though Chris and myself were reasonably confident that the Blackthorn would be successful, it's fair to say that it took off far more quickly than we could have imagined. With a fair degree of publicity and word of mouth, the Blackthorn was soon attracting massive crowds. We often had a line outside the pub on weekends, with 60 people queuing up each side of the door. It was absolutely chock-a-bloc. The lads from the football clubs would come up with their friends. We managed to tap into those people who emigrated from Ireland in the 1980s. Pretty soon, we had a strong base of regular customers, weekend drinkers and a smattering of celebrities who added a certain amount of glamour to the pub.

***

During that era, of course, there was still an abundance of 'illegals' in Boston, and many of them came to the Blackthorn. One day, the American television news channel, CNN, came down to South Boston to film a feature about the green card amnesty for illegals living in America. CNN reporter John Holliman interviewed Mayor Ray Flynn – who would frequently slip into us for a pint – and other people in the area. They also wanted to interview me and a few other people in the bar. The crew spent the entire day with me, sank a few pints in the bar and interviewed illegals, whom they silhouetted because of their status. Our barman Peter Farrell, who was then without a green card, spoke of his own situation.

We were all excited at the prospect of seeing ourselves on CNN the next day, but the finished script was a bit different from what we had been led to expect. The introduction to the piece ran as follows: 'The Blackthorn Bar in South Boston – a haven for Irish "illegals".' There was plenty of slagging and a bit of tension for a couple of days after, with lads running in all directions in case immigration officers turned up. But it soon settled down and the lads kept coming in.

Later, I met the head of the city's immigration service, Bill Whelan, whose people came from Ireland. He told me they always knew what was going on. 'I could have gone down and got two lads to stand at the front door and two at the back door, and I could probably have arrested 80 per cent of the customers,' said Bill. I'd say he wasn't too far off with his figures. Other bars around

Dorchester, such as the Blarney Stone, had similar numbers of illegals as customers.

The Blackthorn provided a social service for those who didn't possess a green card and social security number and needed a 'bank' to cash their cheques. The names on those cheques might have been slightly 'unusual' and not have matched the person cashing it, but we didn't mind, so long as the cheques were okay. Some bounced but we overcame that and made sure we weren't caught again.

Naturally enough, there was always the fear that the illegals could be caught. But in comparison to the way things are today, it was very relaxed. We were very lucky because we had a great mayor in Boston at the time in Ray Flynn, who was one of our own. Ray really looked after the Irish and helped many people to get their green card. The lack of social insurance for illegals meant that there were problems if they needed to go to hospital. Ray did a deal with the City Hospital in Boston: if any illegals were admitted the city would take care of their bills.

***

'Southie' is a different place these days. It's full of new yuppie bars. The Irish lads aren't really welcome in these places, because they like to go in after work with their dirty boots on. But we have no intention of changing the Blackthorn, where the workingman will always be served.

6

WHITEY CALLS BY

IN late 1991, I was recovering from the break up of my marriage to Ann and doing my best to make sure the children weren't too upset. I was also concentrating on building up the clientele of the Blackthorn, which was now heading towards its first birthday. There weren't too many opportunities for nights out, but Chris and Brendan would sometimes join me for a few scoops. It was at the end of one of these fairly low-key sessions that I ended up in the police cells for seven hours. From the outset, I must stress that I was completely the innocent party. I was simply in the wrong place at the wrong time, but the experience made me very angry.

One night, Brendan and myself were enjoying a few pints in the Blackthorn. We decided to call down to Brendan's place, Cuchulainns, to meet up with his business partner, Mike Hanley. When we arrived, the place was fairly quiet. However, there were two lads who seemed to be having a bit of an argument. We paid little or no heed to them, although at one stage Mike did have to come out from behind the counter to break up what appeared to be a harmless tussle. After that, one of the guys left the bar.

A couple of minutes later, you couldn't hear yourself think with the wailing of police sirens outside the pub. We later learned that the bloke who had just left the bar was a police officer who could not hold his drink. He had phoned his colleagues at the station with a false complaint. There were so many police there, that he must have given them the key information 'officer down', which is the worst call that any station can receive. Within seconds of us first hearing the sirens, police were swarming in the front door with their batons and guns at the ready and shouting at us to finish our drinks. There was still half an hour left before closing time, so I knew it wasn't a raid. I raised my glass to finish my drink; just as I lowered it back down onto the counter, I received an unmerciful blow to the face from one of the officers. He then pushed my head on to the counter and handcuffed my hands behind my back.

As I was escorted to the back of the police car, Brendan and Mike both pleaded with the officer in charge, telling him that I was not involved in the earlier incident. Brendan was thrown out the front door of his own pub, while Mike was warned that if came to the police station to bail me out, he, too, would end up in the cells. The officers brought me down to Gibson Street station in Dorchester. They emptied my pockets, and did a double take when they found $800. I was then questioned as to whether I had got the money from selling drugs or robbing somebody!

I wondered if I was in the middle of some dreadful nightmare, but when I was stripped to my underpants and locked up in a cold, dirty cell I knew it was for real. Well, I thought, I'll be given back everything in the morning and I will receive an apology. But the bizarre episode continued when I was ferried up to Dorchester court in a police wagon and thrown into a cell with about 20 of the meanest looking dudes I had ever set eyes on. With $800 now back in my pocket, I wondered if they would tear me apart. After going to the toilet, this big, black guy wandered over to me as he was pulling up his zip and enquired: 'Hey white boy, what you in for?' It was a time for quick thinking, so I replied, 'My name is Frank, and I kicked the f*** out of two white cops last night'. The cell just exploded with laughter, and I was doing high fives for the next two minutes. 'Man, you're all right for a honky,' I was informed. I realised that I was safe, but I still couldn't wait to get the hell out of the cell.

Incredibly, I was hauled up before the court and charged with assaulting a police officer! The arresting officer had alleged that I had attacked him, even though I had not seen him coming to hit me. The lawyer Chris had hired for me entered a not guilty plea. More than a few influential people in the city wanted me to lodge a lawsuit for assault against the cop concerned. I felt that might not be in the best interests of the Blackthorn. Instead, the officer dropped the charges. I had to pay $50 to get the case struck out and to make sure that I would not have a criminal record. It was a lesson in life that still makes me furious.

***

That period of my life seemed to be packed with incidents, quite apart from the family and business drama of daily existence in Southie. A few months earlier, I had had another memorable experience. Saturday 1 June, 1991, wasn't just notable as the date that Ireland played its first senior football international match against the US on American soil. It also turned out to be the date that I first came into contact with Whitey Bolger, one of the FBI's most-wanted men.

In front of a crowd of 51,000 in Foxboro Stadium, Ireland drew 1–1 with the US. After the game, I volunteered to drive a few of the Irish press corps back to their hotel, via the Blackthorn. The lads were glad to get a lift back into town, as it was proving near impossible to hail a cab for the 25-mile journey. At about 11 pm, Peter Byrne of *The Irish Times*, Charlie Stuart of the *Irish Press* and Cathal Dervan of the *Irish Star* had just arrived with me at the bar, when a white car pulled up beside us. The window rolled down and voice from the front passenger seat enquired: 'Frank Gillespie?'

'Yeah.'

'How are you doing?' he asked, as a hand came out the window.

'Good, how are you?' I replied.

'I'm Whitey Bolger.'

'Whitey who?' said I back to him, knowing full well of his reputation in the crime world.

'See all those Irish guys and girls coming over here and going to your bar? You're doing a great job. Keep them all coming over because that's what I like to see.'

When I got back into my own car, Peter asked me whether had I seen a ghost. I told him that I might as well have encountered one. I didn't sleep a wink that night, as I had no idea what the consequences of this 'chat' would be. The next day, I went in to my partner Chris and explained that I had been approached by Whitey and that he had wished us luck. I told Chris that I had a sneaking suspicion that Whitey was going to tap us for something. If that happened, we'd have to get out of the bar business. But as time went on, we were not approached, although we were always a bit wary of the situation. Then one morning, Chris and myself went into a diner to have our breakfast. Whitey was there with a few friends, and said: 'Good morning, Mr Barrett, good morning Mr Gillespie.' 'Good morning, gentlemen,' we replied. When we went up to pay for our breakfast, the bill had already been sorted out. We were wary for another couple of weeks but nothing ever materialised. Through the grapevine, we heard that Whitey was very proud of all the Irish who were flocking to Boston.

**

As the months grew into years, the Blackthorn became firmly established as one of Boston's leading bars. Its reputation spread right across the States and to every county in Ireland. As a result, we began to welcome a wide range of famous names in through the front door. Many of them were Irish, with the balance made up of Irish-Americans and other Americans. Musicians, sportsmen and women, politicians, actors and business people were all welcome on West Broadway.

During the 1994 World Cup finals, I met Albert Reynolds, who was Taoiseach at the time, at a party in New York with Jack Charlton. Albert promised to drop into the Blackthorn. The visit was scheduled for the night after Ireland's 1–0 win over Italy.

However, it was postponed, after loyalists murdered six Irish fans, who were watching the match on television in a pub in County Down. Albert came down the following Monday, and bought everybody a drink. I felt that that was a very generous gesture for a man who doesn't touch a drop of alcohol himself.

His cabinet colleague, Máire Geoghegan-Quinn, dropped in another night, accompanied by Conor O'Riordan, the Irish Consul General in Boston. I knew Conor very well, and he worked hard for the Irish in the city. Máire stayed for two hours and was fantastically friendly, in the true Galway fashion. Being the politician she then was, she went around and shook hands with everybody. The customers had a lot of time for her.

Then there was Brendan O'Carroll. His arrival in Boston began with a phone call from a guy I didn't know. He asked me: 'Would you be interested in taking this comedian from Ireland? His name is Brendan O'Carroll.'

'Never heard of him,' I replied.

'Oh, he's huge in Ireland and all the younger crowd would know him,' came the sales pitch down the phone.

This agent was looking for big money for Brendan – three grand or close to it. 'I can't afford to pay Brendan O'Carroll three grand – sure he's not even known,' I reasoned. We eventually did a deal for $1,500.

I remember the first night very well, because Brendan almost didn't make it onto the stage! There was a cellar door in the kitchen, and as Brendan made his way up to the front of the bar he disappeared straight down the hatch. For a few dreadful moments, I thought he was dead and my heart stopped beating. But, being as agile as he is, Brendan bounced back up, and there wasn't a bother on him. He went on to do a fantastic show. Over the next two or three years, I got him lots of gigs around Boston. He always maintained that he had done so well in the Blackthorn he would always come back for $1,500.

Liam Reilly and Bagatelle were absolutely fantastic and always put on a great show for us. The Barleycorn always packed them in, as did Paddy Reilly. The legendary Phil Coulter also came down to see us. I actually brought Phil shopping once to Filene's Basement in Boston, and afterwards we went for a meal before coming back to enjoy a drink in the Blackthorn. As we supped a few pints, Phil wandered over to the jukebox. I don't know how many of the songs on it he had either written himself or co-written. It was fascinating to learn about his involvement in the music business. Other guests who enjoyed a pint with us at the Blackthorn included Mike Scott and the Waterboys, American rock star Bonnie Raitt and *Star Trek* actor Colm Meaney.

***

Thankfully, the customers and friends we've entertained down through the years have far outnumbered the small handful of idiots and troublemakers we've encountered. Most were simply the worse for wear, but there were also a couple of dangerous characters. During the mid-1990s, Mike Townsend – Andy's brother – was working for us. One day, Chris told him not to serve a particular fella, who was not too happy about the decision. 'The next time I come back I'll be served,' he promised, as he walked out the door. About fifteen minutes later, he came back with four lads. One of them had a gun and went over to Chris and Mike and said: 'So, you're not going to serve my friend?'

Chris confirmed his stand by saying, 'I'm the owner here and I instructed the bartender not to serve your friend'.

'You'll serve him now,' the bloke threatened, sticking the gun in Chris' side.

'Well, if you think by shooting me he'll get a drink, you go ahead but I won't serve him,' Chris replied.

The guy with the gun looked at Chris and at Mike, who was shaking behind the counter. Thankfully, these blokes got the message and the stand-off ended without anybody getting hurt. The hardman put the gun back in his pocket and left the bar.

To this day, we haven't served your man. We didn't get the police involved because he had a few Italian buddies who might have wanted to frighten us. We did receive sort of an apology, and we didn't want to the word to get out on the street that there had been a firearm incident in the Blackthorn.

In the Blackthorn's early days, we also had to take a firm line with clients who we would have preferred drank elsewhere. When we first moved in, there were an awful lot of drugs in South Boston. There was no other option during the first three months but to throw lads out left, right and centre in order to clean the place up. Not surprisingly, I was threatened on many occasions. One night, a fella who was barred parked his truck facing towards the front door, ready to drive through it. Luckily enough, the cops arrived in time and sorted him out. But that didn't deter him, and he called down one night and pointed a gun through the window. In the end, we had to get police protection.

***

With the Blackthorn ticking along so well, in 1999 Chris and myself felt it was the right time to purchase another bar in Boston. We looked around for a while and finally settled on a place by the name of Deeney O'Malley's. It needed a lot of work. We thought we'd spend $60,000 to $80,000 on doing it up, stage by stage. But when we started to do the preliminary work, the place fell apart. The renovation was now turning into a complete reconstruction. I lost count of the skip loads of rubbish we wheeled out of the pub.

During the late 1990s, all of Boston's motorways were being put underground. This became known as the 'big dig' and was one of the most ambitious civil engineering projects ever embarked upon anywhere in the world. Word spread around Boston's other bars that things were not as they seemed at Deeney O'Malley's. Soon, the wags in other pubs were calling the rebuilding of the Baggot Inn – that's the name we went for in honour of the Dublin venue – the 'big dig'.

The Boston Baggot was a four-storey-high building. From the first floor up, there was nothing left standing but the four walls. We had to rebuild it, the whole way up. Without John Kavanagh, our carpenter, we'd have been lost. Carlow-born John had emigrated to Boston during the 1980s, with nothing to his name. He quickly got into the building business, and there is no doubt that he is the finest carpenter I have ever come across. John stuck with us as the extent of the project unfolded. Every morning that I came into the pub, John would inform me that something else was wrong. I'd tell him, 'Keep going, John, there's nothing we can do but to keep going.' We worked at it day and night from February to August 1999.

On the night that we finally and successfully opened the Boston Baggot on 7 August, 1999, John's great gibe to us was 'Keep going'! But we had to overcome one last hitch that threatened the opening. About 5 o'clock that evening, the health inspector came into me while everybody was going around finishing up the last bits and pieces of decorating. After a quick glance around the pub, she refused to give me the licence to open up. From our point of view, all was fine, but she found that the lads were still tidying off a few pieces of wiring. I firmly believe it was little more than bureaucracy.

I pleaded with her, and she finally relented by saying: 'I'll give you one chance and if I come back in here and everybody's out of the place and all the last bits and pieces are done, I'll consider giving you a licence to open up.' Well, you never saw such a scattering match in all your life. Within minutes, everybody was out of there with everything tidied up. She came back and gave us the go-ahead. As soon as she was gone, everybody was back in there doing the last bits and pieces again.

Kevin Moran came over to officially open the pub. He was joined by two other former Dublin Gaelic football greats, Jack Sheedy and Fran Ryder. Kevin was his usual friendly and accommodating self. Chris and myself handed him an envelope to pay him for coming over, but it was thrown back at us. 'We've been friends for years and this is something I want to do for you,' said Kevin. That level of generosity was typical of the man.

We enjoyed a couple of good years in the Boston Baggot, but the outflow of the immigrants back to Ireland meant that we had fewer customers. It got to the stage where we felt we were splitting our crowd between the Baggot and the Blackthorn. So when we received a good offer for the Baggot, we just let it go. Chris and myself are now concentrating our efforts on the Blackthorn; it's great that the pub can still pack them in.

These days, however, business is not as good as it once was during the 1990s. There are now so many pubs in Boston that competition is getting tougher all the time. The 9/11 tragedy that affected so many people bit the Blackthorn as well. With the introduction of new security laws, there has been a big clampdown on illegals, who have been the backbone of our business since we opened in 1990. Many of them have gone home to Ireland, while others have moved on to different parts of the world.

The crackdown on the Irish in the US is really resented. I wouldn't say that there will be too many Irish people voting Republican in the presidential election in November. Times have even changed in local city politics, with Ray Flynn now departed from his office as Mayor of Boston. We don't even have an Irish mayor any more; Tom Menino, an Italian, is now mayor of the 33rd county of Ireland. Southie was once known for the rivalry between the Irish and Italian communities, but that day has passed and the two groups now get on well.

7

THE FUREYS STAND BY ME

FROM my earliest days in the pram in Tyrrellspass, I have never been too far away from music. Be it my late mother or father singing a ballad at home or listening to a CD as I drive, music has been a constant source of pleasure and companionship to me. There's nothing I like better than enjoying a singsong in the Blackthorn over a pint or attending a concert by a group, be they Irish, American or from another corner of the planet.

Many famous musicians have visited the Blackthorn. My connections in the music business have created opportunities for me that my own singing voice could never have hoped to deliver.

I have always loved Irish music, and I suppose when I left Ireland, I came to love it all the more. I have to thank Finbar Furey, of the famous Fureys, for getting me involved in the music business. In the 18 or so years that I've known Finbar and the other fellas from the band – George, Eddie and the late Paul – I have travelled the length and breath of Ireland in their company and also toured the States and Australia with them. In the course of my travels, I have enjoyed the company of the then Taoiseach, Albert Reynolds, and saw the lads cross verbal swords with another Irish politician, the controversial Padraig 'Pee' Flynn.

My entry into the Irish music industry began through my late, great friend, Tommy McGann, who owned the Irish Embassy pub in Easton, about 40 minutes outside Boston near Cape Cod. The Irish Embassy was one of the first pubs to bring bands like the Dubliners and the Fureys over to the States in the mid to late

1980s. A group of us often hired a bus and got a crowd of 40 or 50 people from Boston to go down and support Tommy. Afterwards, Tommy and myself would usually end up having a pint with the musicians.

I became great friends with the Fureys, the Dublin City Ramblers and the Dubliners. One night, the Blackthorn staff was having an after-hours pint with two local police officers. We heard a rattle from one of the shutters, which were down. One of the cops took out his gun, because we were all afraid that someone was trying to break in. The shutters were opened fairly quickly. All I could hear was, 'Don't shoot – it's only the Dublin City Ramblers. We're looking for a pint!' I brought the lads in and told them: 'There's only one way you'll get a pint here tonight, lads. You'll have to sing a song.' Singer Patsy Watchorn quickly replied: 'Who's going to stop us?' We stayed until the early hours of the morning, singing with the policemen and the Dublin City Ramblers.

After one memorable show by the Fureys, I told them that I was thinking of buying a pub. They promised that if I ever did, they'd open it for me. The Fureys were as good as their word. In October 1990, a few months after the Blackthorn actually opened its doors for business, the lads played a gig to 'officially' launch the bar. Our friendship grew steadily, and after a while they asked me if I'd be able to book a few gigs for them. I ended up doing some promotional work and tour management for the Fureys across America.

In the middle of 1991, Finbar was over in Boston and invited me to tour with them early the following year in Australia and New Zealand. The invitation was just the lift I needed, as I was very down over the break up of my marriage to Ann. Finbar thought it would do me good if I came away with them for a stint. I spoke to Chris about it, and he was completely supportive. So, off I headed, meeting up with the Fureys in London in February 1992. But as often seems to be the way with me, I almost didn't make it to Oz.

The night before the flight from Heathrow, I stayed in my sister's house. I was supposed to get a train from Wimbledon station out to the airport. That morning, an IRA bomb went off in Wimbledon station. I actually heard the blast when I was in the house, getting ready to leave for the airport. I had to jump in a cab and tell the driver to get me to the airport as quickly as possible. The traffic was chaotic because of the blast, and I made it to the terminal with minutes to spare.

I joined Eddie, Paul, George and Finbar Furey, Francie Conway (who was filling in for Davy Arthur who had left the Fureys at the time) and the crew, Tommy Murtagh and Billy Gorman. On the flight over, I was told all sorts of stories about the lads' fame in Australia, but I didn't really appreciate it until we got there and saw the number of people waiting for them at Sydney airport.

Even the long-haul journey to Sydney wasn't without incident. During the stopover on the British Airways' flight, we had a couple of hours to kill in Singapore, so we enjoyed a few scoops. Francie had written a song called 'Barney Here from the County Clare', which we all kept singing. The airport police weren't very happy with our conduct and warned us in no uncertain way that, if we didn't quieten down, this would be the end of our trip. 'Barney' was put on hold until we landed in Australia, whereupon the song was resurrected. We sang it so often that the tour manager thought that Barney was one of the crew!

I think the lads got a bit of a laugh out of it all, as it reminded them of an incident during their first tour of Australia. One night, Davy Arthur and the late Paul Furey were having a quick 'leak' at the back of the club they were playing in. Some cops caught them and wanted to arrest them for urinating in the street. It ended up in a bit of a free for all, and the boys were brought to jail. They made the headlines big time in Ireland and Australia, where it was carried on national TV. The matter ended up in court, and the boys were fined several thousand Australian dollars. However, the judge allowed them to donate their fine to a charity of their choice. They gave the money to homeless kids. Since then, at every concert they play in Australia, the Fureys have a collection for homeless children.

My role on the tour was concert MC. The Fureys are fiercely proud of their roots. Before the first gig, I received a strict warning that when I was introducing the lads I had to say that they were from Ballyfermot. I'd go out on stage and say: 'Ladies and gentlemen, put your hands together for Ireland's greatest ambassadors, all the way from Ballyfermot in County Dublin, the world-famous Fureys.'

The Fureys' popularity around the world is amazing. They play to full houses in Ireland, but when they play in Australia, the US, Germany and Holland, there is even greater demand for tickets. I remember one day walking with the lads through the streets of Sydney. We had to get them into taxis and send them back to the hotel, because such massive crowds had gathered around them.

One of Oz's best-known radio DJs, Burt Newton, has long been a massive fan of the lads and was once scolded by his producer for playing 'Sweet 16' three times in one morning! In 1992, Burt was hosting his own breakfast show on Australian television, so naturally he invited a few of the lads on. I accompanied George and Finbar to the studios, when they sprang a surprise on me. 'I believe that you have a young man travelling with you who owns a bar in Boston,' enquired Burt. The camera turned to focus on me, and I found myself being interviewed by Burt Newton.

'How're the Kennedys doing over there? You know Ted Kennedy?' Burt asked.

I said, 'Yeah, he's been into the pub once or twice.'

Burt went on: 'I believe he got married.'

I said, 'Aw yeah, Ted's been known to drop the pants a few times!'

Burt chuckled and moved on quickly: 'This guy is quite a character, isn't he? I hope this isn't being picked up in Boston,' he added. 'The possibility is that we'll all face lawsuits!'

That, of course, gave the Fureys the perfect opportunity to stage one of their regular stunts. A few nights later, we were at a concert venue when two Australian policemen handed me an envelope. 'It's a lawsuit from Ted Kennedy. We'll have to take you down to the station,' one of them said. I was raging for a while, but the lads were over in a corner having a great laugh.

The next chance for some innocent fun arose on another breakfast TV show. I usually roomed with Finbar, and one night after a show we arrived back at the hotel at about two o'clock in the morning. Five hours later, I got a belt of a pillow and was told to get up and get into the shower as we had a bit of work to do. Warned not to ask any questions, I did what I was told. I went outside, where a car was waiting for us. During the journey, I kept saying, 'Where are we going?' 'Don't be asking questions,' Finbar told me. I eventually found myself in a studio, lying back on a chair and getting make-up put on me. Finally, the sweat started to come out through me.

'You're going to have to tell me what's going on, Finbar.'

'Paul and Eddie weren't too well this morning. We were all supposed to cook an Irish stew on *Good Morning Australia*. Now you're doing it with me. You're Frankie Furey!'

So, Frankie Furey — the behind-the-scenes and introverted brother — was wheeled out on national television. We ended up cooking a great Irish stew for St Patrick's Day, which was two days later. And believe you me, it was some stew! Finbar explained that it was lamb stew with loads of garlic in it, because garlic, he said, grows wild in Ireland. The appearance was going fine, until just before end, the presenter, Colette Mann, turned around to me and asked: 'And what do you play, Frankie?'

The Blackthorn Bar tricolour flies proudly at Giants Stadium, New Jersey, on Saturday, 18 June, 1994, during Ireland's 1–0 World Cup victory over Italy.

My mother's Alice's family, the O'Connors of Meedin, County Westmeath.

My mother and myself pictured on a visit to our cousins, the Magees,
in Mullingar. I'm aged 7.

My dad, 'the Colonel', in command.

The Gillespie family L–R (Back) Eileen, Lolo, Massey, 'the Colonel',
Kathleen, Claire, Marion.
(Front) Frank, John, James, Michael, Vincent, Eugene.

Finbar Furey enjoying a pint in the Blackthorn.

The Fureys' tour of America in 1992 took us to the world-famous
Carnegie Hall in New York.

Big Jack enjoying a well-earned pint amongst family and friends in the Blackthorn during his 60th birthday celebrations in Boston in May 1995.

Big Jack's 'arrest' by members of the Boston Police Department.

Me with Dublin All-Ireland senior football medal winner, Jack Sheedy and dual soccer and Gaelic football legend, Kevin Moran, who officially opened the Baggot Inn in Boston in August 1999.

Here, I'm flanked by Jack Charlton and Roy Keane at the dinner after Denis Irwin's Manchester United testimonial against Manchester City in August 2000.

*Roy Keane having a chat with my girlfriend, Melanie (left) and my
daughter, Donna, at the Holiday Inn Hotel, Dublin airport.*

*Roy Keane's parents, Marie and Mossie, enjoyed a great
holiday with me in Boston. Here they are relaxing
over a drink in Ned Kelly's bar in Boston.*

By mid–1993, I had been appointed social officer to the Ireland football squad. At Dublin airport in June that year, I discussed the forthcoming trips to Riga in Latvia and Vilnius in Lithuania with Kevin Moran and Ray Houghton.

Denis Irwin and U2's sound engineer Joe O'Herlihy join in Manchester United's league victory celebrations in May 1993.

Ireland and Galway Gaelic football physio, Mick Byrne, and Galway hero, Jarlath Fallon, with me after the Tribesmen's historic Sam Maguire win over Kildare in 1998.

David Beckham and myself at Denis Irwin's testimonial match at Old Trafford in August 2000.

I always found alex Ferguson to be really friendly. Here, I met him during Denis Irwin's testimonial match.

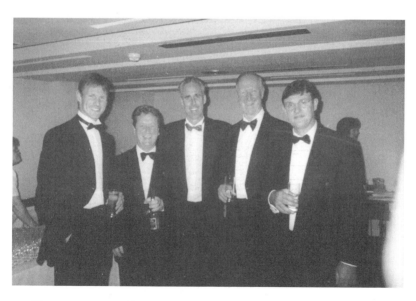

They all turned out for Denis Irwin's testimonial game and dinner: (L–R) Teddy Sheringham, myself, Mick McCarthy, Jack Charlton and Kevin Moran.

This is a photograph I will always treasure. I was fortunate to meet former Manchester United manager Matt Busby in Manchester in December 1993, just six weeks before he passed away at the age of 85.

Melanie and myself enjoying a few drinks in McGann's bar in Boston, a few months after the horrific accident that left Melanie seriously injured.

With the apples of my eye, daughter Donna and son Trevor.

Michael Flatley's engagement party to his then girlfriend Lisa Murphy was a lavish affair at his home in Nice. Here we take a moment off.

Of all the famous people who've walked through the front door of the Blackthorn, boxer Jake La Motta of Raging Bull *fame must rank with the best.*

John Smith, Steve Collins, Frank Smith and myself after the press conference to announce the world title fight between Steve and Chris Eubank in Millstreet, Cork, in March 1995.

There's no disguising my excitement after Ireland's 1–0 World Cup win over Italy in June 1994. Larry Mullen is taking it all in his stride.

Former Westmeath and Tyrellspass Gaelic football great, Mick Carley, and myself proudly show off the Westmeath senior football championship cup after the Tyrellspass win in 1999.

London minor football team-mate John Barry (right) and myself on the famous Croke Park turf following our All-Ireland minor championship defeat by Cavan in July 1974.

Colm Meaney has 'beamed' himself down to the Blackthorn on a few occasions.

The picture that says it all about Manchester United's 1998–99 season. The European Cup, FA Cup and Premiership trophies sit in front of Jack Charlton, your's truly and Alex Ferguson.

John Aldridge, Frank Smith, co-owner of the Submarine Bar in Dublin, and myself.

'I play everything and the Guinness!' I replied. To which Finbar turned around and added, 'The Guinness bottle and the spoons'.

We got away with it. The station must have been quite happy too, as they repeated that segment on St Patrick's Day. A couple of days later, I was in Adelaide with the lads who were signing autographs. One fella came up to me and said: 'I saw you on *Good Morning Australia* the other day. You're Frankie Furey. My wife made that stew for me the other day and she nearly poisoned me.' So, I backed off, went out the back door and headed up to the pub where we had a great laugh. I still have a video of that performance and it never fails to raise a chuckle.

St Patrick's Day saw us in Melbourne, where the lads played a concert at four o'clock to 4,200 people in the Melbourne Concert Hall, and then did another show at nine o'clock that was also packed out. On the morning of those shows, we bumped into one Pee Flynn of Castlebar at a breakfast reception in the Hilton Hotel, which was hosted by the Australian Prime Minister, Paul Keating. Pee Flynn was his usual bubbly self and insisted on getting into all the photographs. For most people present, the Fureys were the main attraction, not the County Mayo politician. The lads were a bit browned off. When Flynn light-heartedly advised them to 'keep the tax man happy', Eddie let rip. 'The best thing you can do is to build a jail for the politicians – we paid our own way here, unlike you.'

One night, we were in a pub in Sydney when we spotted Denis Waterman, the famous English actor from *Minder*. Denis was having a bit of a hard time over in a corner, because people were hassling him for autographs and photographs. We went up and rescued him by inviting him down to our cornered-off part of the bar. 'The Fureys?' he said. 'Oh, my God, I was looking at yez this morning on television.' We all agreed that we'd meet up for a game of golf the following morning. Unfortunately, the Guinness affected Denis and he sent his apologies!

Golf was a major source of relaxation for the boys, and they tried to get in as many rounds as possible during the trip. At one particular course, the owners were reluctant to waive the green fees in return for publicity from the boys. Finbar then introduced me as Ian Woosnam, and immediately the red carpet was rolled onto the first tee! Thanks be to God, my opening drive sailed right down the fairway and Woosie was able to continue signing autographs.

The eight weeks on the road brought us all around the amazing continent of Australia. We played in old mining towns in the centre of the country, as well as many of the biggest venues in Melbourne, Sydney, Adelaide and Perth. Then we departed for Christchurch, Wellington and Auckland in New Zealand and the Tasmanian cities of Hobart and Launceston. After the shows, we often met people who had travelled for as long two days to see the Fureys.

One night in Auckland, a Limerickman came over to me outside the hall and told me that he was opening up an Irish pub that night in the city. He asked me how much it would cost to have the lads up for half an hour. The lads accepted the invite free of charge, as there were a few 'free gargles' in it for them. Finbar even announced it on stage during the gig. We arrived in the back door of the pub and ended up behind the counter. We gave them a blast of 'Barney Here from the County Clare'. When we were leaving, the owner actually cried because he was so delighted with the success of the night.

The late Paul Furey was in his element on that tour. I was in Seoul, South Korea, in 2002 when I heard that he had died. He was a lovely fellow, who was possessed of great humour and just lived for his music. It was Paul who showed me how to play the spoons; he even made me a set of them once. He made them so well – they wouldn't slip off your fingers – that he stole them back off me and it was only two years later that I realised it!

Paul's love of telling a story would have any audience spellbound. If you ever wanted to know where Paul was in a bar, you just had to look for the greatest crowd of people. One night in Australia, he told one of his great stories: While digging in his back garden, Paul came across the wing of an aeroplane. He rang Finbar, Eddie and George and told them to give him a hand to dig it out. The assembled Aussies said: 'Go 'way, mate, go 'way.'

Paul went on, 'We started to dig and kept digging until about 10 o'clock that night when we found a World War II aeroplane.'

'What'd you do with it, mate?' asked one of the Aussies.

'Well, we got it lifted up and I had an old Volkswagen at home, so I took the engine out of the plane and I put it into the Volkswagen. I'm flying around Dublin in it now,' he quipped.

'And where's the other part, mate, where's the shell?' asked the Aussies.

'Oh, that's hanging in the history museum in Dublin and, if you ever go there, our name is on it!'

Another night on the same tour, a fella challenged Paul to a storytelling competition, with a crate of beer as the prize. The bartender was appointed the judge. The bloke said: 'Go ahead, tell me the best story you have.' You could have heard a pin drop. Paul said: 'No, no, you're challenging me, you go ahead.'

So the fella said: 'Well, I was in Canada one time when I took off all my clothes, jumped into Niagara Falls and swam up it backways!'

Paul retorted: 'Yeah, I know, I saw you.' So he stuck your man to the ground and there was no comeback. Paul got the crate of beer.

During the tour Down Under, I got a glimpse of what a talented songwriter Finbar is. When we were en route from one part of Australia to another, Finbar wrote the first two verses of a song and then stopped, as he couldn't think of any more words. A few nights later in the hotel room, I got a dig.

'What's wrong?' I said.

'Have you any steamers on you, Sham?' he asked − steamers being cigarettes.

'I have, there's some there in me pocket.'

'Get up with me quick,' he said, 'because we're going to have a little drop of whiskey. I'm just after dreaming about the other two verses.'

We got up and had a glass of whiskey and a couple of steamers. Finbar put pen to paper and completed the other two verses, and we went back to bed very happy.

On the way home from the tour, we stopped in Bangkok. We had already taken loads of drink. Another stirring singsong started in the bar in Bangkok airport. The authorities thought that we were too lubricated, and a series of negotiations were needed for us to get back on the plane. We were lucky, as a few months earlier the authorities had locked up a 'tired and emotional' Australian rugby team for the night.

At the time of the Australian tour, my mother wasn't well. Finbar was always very kind to her. Before and after the tour, he came down, sat on the side of her bed and gave her advice on how to get better. My mother never drank in her life, but Finbar insisted that she should drink two glasses of whiskey a day. She actually tried to drink the whiskey. He also wrote her a lovely poem, which she had hanging over her bed. It was basically a story about the heartbreak that she had endured when I emigrated to America. My mother fell in love with this poem – as I did myself. When my mother passed away on 9 October, 1992, we put it on her gravestone in Tyrrellspass cemetery:

Lonely without you, she sometimes cries.
I feel her pain, lonely without you.
I sometimes cry, but for her tears, for the pain you left,
* for the tears you never see,*
For the heart wounded there,
A heart I can never mend, a heart that needs my tears.

***

Later, I toured many parts of America with the Fureys – down into New Orleans, Texas and Florida, then up to New York. Anywhere that we could get a gig and there were loads of Irish to be entertained, we were there. For one of their gigs, the lads were playing at the world-famous Carnegie Hall in New York, with the English comedian, Tom O'Connor, opening for them. We were all staying in Fitzpatrick's Hotel in the city. The night before the gig, we met the Clancy Brothers and enjoyed an all-nighter with them.

At about one o'clock in the afternoon on the day of the concert, Finbar and myself came down the elevator in Fitzpatricks. There was an awful commotion in the foyer and the place was packed with plainclothes police and FBI officers. We were blocked from getting off the elevator. And who was it, only Albert Reynolds walking in the main door. Finbar shouted: 'Ah, it's only Albert Reynolds. Jesus, Albert, they'd let anyone in here.' The cops overreacted and got into a bit of a panic, but Albert said, 'Ah, no, that's okay. I know that man, that's Finbar Furey.' He walked over to Finbar and they had a chat. Finbar then asked the Taoiseach to introduce the band on stage in Carnegie Hall at 3.30 that afternoon. Albert promised that he'd do his best, and he was as good as his word.

By the time we got out of the hall after the gig, there was another show due on, so people were lining up outside. I took off my jacket, threw it on the ground and the lads got out their guitars and began to busk. An old lady threw a dollar bill onto the coat, shook our hands and said: 'You guys are very good, and if you keep this up, some day you might even be in there.'

'Sure, we're only after coming out of that kip, missus,' replied Eddie.

The Furey's ability to have a laugh with people is probably as important to their success as their music. Without one, the other would be far less telling. That mixture of musical appeal and easy-going Irish friendliness is summed up by their long-standing relationship with Geraldine Chaplin, the daughter of comedian Charlie Chaplin. Years ago, the band was invited to play at the Charlie Chaplin charity golf classic in Waterville, County Kerry. Geraldine was there and fell in love with their music. She gave them one of their father's songs. George recorded it with a full orchestra, and the Fureys sometimes play it at their concerts.

Thirty years after they started entertaining us, the Fureys are still on the road, although Davy Arthur and Finbar only gig with them on certain occasions. The Furey brothers are deeply talented and know how to entertain. They enjoy talking and arguing about music and have incredibly high standards. Larry Mullen of U2 once said to me: 'We had to learn music; the Fureys were born with it.'

8

BIG JACK'S BIRTHDAY BASH

B IG Jack is a very special person whose ability to relate to and deal with people was the basis of his success as manager of the Irish football team. To his detractors, the Geordie may come across as gruff and uncompromising but, to those who have been fortunate enough to know him well, he is a true gentleman. In the 13 years that I have known him, he has been a man content with his lot and happy to help those around him.

During the 1992 US Cup and the 1994 World Cup finals, my relationship with Jack blossomed. From then on, we were in regular contact by telephone and met up frequently in England and Ireland. In May 1995, Jack decided to spend his 60th birthday in Boston. It gave me the ideal opportunity to honour the man who had revolutionised Irish football. After chatting with a few close friends, I opted to organise a surprise gala dinner for Jack in the downtown Park Plaza Hotel.

At that time, Mike Connolly from Galway was one of the managers at the famous hotel. With just six weeks to go before the big night on Sunday, 7 May, Mike set about organising an occasion to impress the special guest, his family and friends. With the help of Chris Barrett and all the staff at the Blackthorn, I also got my skates on. Lorraine Harris of the Aer Lingus office in Boston sponsored flights for Brendan O'Carroll and his band to fly out from Dublin. The cable television network Celtic Vision offered advertising slots to sell tables at the event. My good friends Liam and Susan Tiernan were not found wanting when it came to elbow grease.

The celebrations actually kicked-off a week before the party, when Jack flew into Boston just after Ireland's 1–0 win over Portugal in their Euro '96 qualifying group. That victory at Lansdowne Road left Ireland odds-on to reach the finals in England – something that Jack really wanted to achieve. Accompanied by his wife, Pat, eldest son, John, and closest acquaintances, Big Jack was in brilliant form. He settled into his suite in the Park Plaza, where Guinness had installed the customary keg of stout in the corner.

The presence of Jack's staff from the international set up was crucial to the success of the bash. Two days before the party, physio Mick Byrne and kit man Charlie O'Leary flew out from Dublin with their wives. I wondered how we could keep them from meeting Jack by chance, because they were all staying in the same hotel. We came up with the perfect solution and sprang a great surprise on Big Jack on the Friday night. With Mike Connolly's assistance, we dressed Mick and Charlie up as hotel chefs and ordered a 'fake' meal from room service. When we told Jack that there were two chefs and a trolley at the door of his suite, he insisted that there must be some mistake. The boys then backed in through the door, turned around and announced: 'Happy birthday, boss!'

I have seen many different expressions, but for sheer joy you could not beat the look on Jack's face. He grabbed Mick and Charlie, hugged and kissed them before falling back into his chair. There wasn't a dry eye in the room, including my own. 'I've never been so caught out in all my life,' Jack cried.

Jack's claim wasn't quite true, because a few days previously we had set him up down in the Blackthorn. That day, I arranged for Jack to be 'arrested' by a few cops I knew. I'm still not sure if he has ever really forgiven me! One afternoon, the two police officers arrived into the pub for a drink and said they were game for a bit of fun. A couple of hours later, Jack was sitting down in the pub enjoying a drink with Pat and a few of his close friends, when the two cops returned. They confronted Jack and informed him that there had been a complaint that he had been drunk and disorderly and insulted someone in the police force. Because of the allegation, they continued, they had no option but to take him downtown for questioning.

Jack was dumbfounded and the blood drained from his face. When he eventually stood up, he said to the two lads: 'No, there's no way; there must be a mistake. Frank, talk to these people.'

'Jesus, Jack, I don't know, I don't know. What did he do?' I asked, as I looked at the two coppers.

'You stay out of it,' I was politely told by my friend. 'He's coming with us.'

By this stage you, could hear a pin drop in the bar. All drinks had been set down as the 'drama' unfolded. The great thing about the wind up was that most of the other people in the bar knew nothing about it. Their expressions turned to near horror when handcuffs were placed on Jack's wrists, and he was brought out of the pub.

I began to feel sorry for Jack. I thought I saw a tear in his eye, and there was no doubt that he was panicking. The officers brought him outside and put him into the car, where I took a few photographs of the 'arrest'. Maybe it was the sight of me with the camera or just that the ludicrous nature of the 'arrest' finally hit home, but Jack eventually realised that it was a set up. His next few words to me contained plenty of 'f***s', but I think he actually got a great kick out of it.

The gala dinner in the Park Plaza was a roaring success, attended by almost 1,000 people from Ireland, England and the US, including politicians, sportsmen and women and media representatives. The Irish Consul General in Boston, Conor O'Riordan, hailed it as one of the best Irish events ever staged in the city. Ted Kennedy, Larry Mullen, Alex Ferguson and Ron Atkinson were amongst those who sent faxes of congratulations.

Fergie simply enquired: 'How vain can a man be to hide in Boston to celebrate his 60th birthday?' Big Ron urged his old managerial adversary not to 'blow your money as you usually do and save some to buy me a drink back home'. When the speeches were finished and the cake was cut, Brendan O'Carroll's band, which included Gerry Browne and Gerry Simpson, entertained us until the wee hours. The night even made the local papers in Boston, and back in Ireland *The Star* ran a fantastic front-page picture of Jack enjoying a pint of stout during the festivities.

After we recovered from the party, I asked Jack to 'do' a TV advert for the Blackthorn. 'No problem, Frank – what's the money like?' asked Jack. I replied to Jack: 'There's no money involved – this is a freebee for me because your birthday cost me a fortune!' Celtic Vision arrived down at the pub and shot Jack pulling pints of Guinness, as Chris and myself walked in the front door. I asked Jack to recommend a drink. 'I normally drink the Guinness myself,' said Jack, who rounded off the 30 seconds by stating: 'Come down to the Blackthorn in South Boston – you never know who'll be pulling the pints!'

Jack finally departed for home a happy man, ready to focus on the rest of the qualifying campaign for Euro '96. Unfortunately within a few weeks, the wheels had come off the wagon with the scoreless draw in Liechtenstein followed by back-to-back 3–1 defeats by Austria. Then the side lost 3–0 away to Portugal in Lisbon, which meant that the team needed to defeat Holland in a play-off in Anfield in December 1995. Two goals from Patrick Kluivert ended that dream, and within a week Jack had stepped down as international team boss.

***

When the Irish government granted Jack his honorary Irish citizenship, I reckon it was one of the few times that the nation's leaders correctly read the will of the people. I was fortunate enough to cover the highways and byways of Ireland with Jack, be it on football business or holidays or on the way to one of his corporate engagements. It was on these journeys that I really saw how the Irish people had taken Jack to their hearts. Old and young, football mad or sports illiterate, they all recognised Jack and wanted to say hello. I think he was sometimes overwhelmed by it all.

Jack loved doing his bit for charity, and was always an enthusiastic attendant at the annual fishing outing for handicapped children in Bantry, County Cork. One year, Jack and I drove through the night from Dublin to ensure that he was present at the event. On arrival, he applied his magic by fixing a rod for a young girl, who promptly caught a 10-pound fish!

Of course, the stories about Jack have become bigger than the reality, particularly the myths about his supposed unwillingness to spend money. One of the most hyped and untrue yarns is that Jack always paid with personal cheques, which he knew would never be cashed, because people wanted to keep his autograph. I only saw Jack pay by cheque once, when he didn't have any cash on him. However, like the fella who caught the five-pound salmon, the story got legs and it soon translated into a 20-pound whopper, with claims that every second shop in Ireland had a Jack Charlton cheque pinned to the wall.

However, what did happen sometimes was that shopkeepers wanted to give Jack things for free. One day, we were in Tarbert in County Kerry, and stopped to buy two choc-ices. When Jack went to pay, the owner said, 'That's on the house, Mr Charlton'. As we walked back to car, Jack turned to me and admitted: 'You know, I'm so well loved in this country it's embarrassing.'

The word embarrassing springs to mind when Jack and myself travelled up to Belfast from Limerick in June 1995. We were going to watch Northern Ireland, who were in the same group as us, play Latvia in a Euro '96 qualifier. Jack had taken the Irish squad down to Limerick for a week's preparations ahead of the ill-fated Liechtenstein and Austria matches. Jack's assistant manager, Maurice Setters, was left in charge of affairs in Limerick.

As it was such a long journey, we stayed overnight in Jack's house in Ballina. After arriving in Belfast early the next morning, we parked in the grounds of a hotel and had a quick kip in the car. By chance, Northern Ireland manager Bryan Hamilton came upon us. He knocked on the window to wake us up and invited us in for tea and sandwiches. Bryan is a gentleman and could not have been more courteous – unlike his predecessor, Billy Bingham. Bingham had exchanged words with Jack during the famous 1–1 draw between the North and the Republic at Windsor Park in November 1993. He wound up the home crowd no end that night. I never encountered so much hatred in one place, so we were all glad to get out of there with the right result.

Northern Ireland lost to Latvia. Jack was privately thrilled, as it gave us a real boost in our group. We left Belfast with a spring in our step. We were running out of petrol, but as we drove west we could not locate a petrol station that was open. The blame game began, with Jack pointing his finger at me and me returning the compliment! After dismissing the idea of stopping at a B&B because of the disruption it would cause to the following day's training regime in Limerick, we pulled into a filling station that was locked up for the night. I was sure that the owner would fill us up with petrol. There was no reply from the house beside the station, but the people in the house next door told us that the owner lived four miles down the road. Just as I returned to the car, an RUC patrol pulled in beside us. Jack began to explain the situation to them. They agreed to bring the owner up to the filling station.

When she arrived, she refused to fill the tank until Jack signed an autograph! With signatures sorted out for her and the RUC officers, we continued our journey to Ballina where, over a glass of whiskey, Jack swore me to secrecy. 'We'd never live it down if that got out,' he said. After training the next day, Jack called me over and blasted: 'I told you to say nothing about running out of petrol – it's all over the *Evening Herald*.' I protested my innocence. It later emerged that the RUC press office had let the public know of its late-night mission in County Tyrone.

The players had a field day over that incident, with Aldo taking real delight in slagging Jack. Jack never likes to be bettered and he got his chance of revenge on Aldo before the week was out. The next day, Jack and I went out to the River Shannon to return a fishing rod to a fella who had loaned it to Jack. When we were there, an angler invited Jack to try his luck, and he reeled in three salmon in the space of an hour. Back in the Castletroy Park Hotel, where the Irish team was based, Jack asked the head chef to put the largest salmon on display, when the players arrived in for their evening meal. As good as his word, the chef presented the prize catch on a silver platter with the words 'Jack's catch today' written underneath. Aldo, who's a keen fisherman, saw the salmon and asked me who had given the fish to Jack. When I told Aldo the truth, he went very quiet. I suppose there are fishermen and fisherboys.

**

My friendship with Jack was threatened by a lazy piece of journalism. Just before the 1994 World Cup finals, the Irish squad was staying at the Forte Post Hotel at Dublin airport. One morning, Jack strode across the lobby with a very concerned look on his face. I immediately knew there was something major bugging him. 'I've just received a phone call from an English reporter who said that you are involved in the IRA,' blurted out Jack. Stunned by Jack's words, it took me a few seconds to regain my composure.

I have never been involved with any type of paramilitary organisation. Slowly, as I reassured Jack of my complete innocence, the penny dropped. Not long before, BBC's *Panorama* had screened a programme about the raising of funds for the IRA in North America, in which the Blackthorn was featured. *Panorama* made no allegations about the Blackthorn, but simply showed the pub because it was such a popular haunt with Irish exiles in the city.

After the broadcast, I had conferred with my lawyers in Boston with regard to an apology and potential compensation from the BBC over the matter. But I soon realised that it would cost me more money to launch a legal case than I could afford at the time.

Jack was quite satisfied with my explanation. He phoned the English journalist back and threatened to sue him if he printed so much as a word of the allegation. Nothing ever appeared. I put the incident down to an attempt to taint Jack and the Ireland side ahead of the World Cup. 'The trouble is, Frank, these people may publish things that are not true and are proven to be untrue,' confided Jack. 'However, some s*** always sticks. I think some of them are intent on doing us an injustice because of our success.'

***

Jack's relationship with the FAI was something of a roller-coaster ride. He was never a great lover of UEFA and FIFA, and I think some of that dislike applied to the boys in Merrion Square. Jack did enjoy a great relationship with certain FAI officers. He regarded former president and honorary secretary Des Casey and the late Charlie Walsh (honorary treasurer) – who were both in charge when he was appointed in 1986 – as friends. On occasion, Pat and Jack stayed with Des and his wife, Mary, in Dundalk.

I think Jack was a bit disappointed that Des was unable to make the meeting of senior FAI officers in December 1995, when Jack was asked to stand down from his post as Ireland manager. Des probably didn't want to be part of the process.

To me, Jack was a thorn in the FAI side. He was his own man, and ran things the way he wanted to. I'd say if they could have got away with it, the FAI would have interfered a lot more in team and squad matters. I thought some of the players were treated like dirt. When I was close to the squad, I saw some of the FAI hierarchy coming into the hotel and not even speaking to the players. There were times when preparations before a match were a shambles. On flights to away games, the blazer brigade sat up front in the best seats on planes, while the players were forced to sit down with the punters. The hotel accommodation wasn't always up to scratch. The North Orlando Hilton Hotel, where the lads were based in Orlando for the 1994 World Cup finals, was not up to scratch as regards sports facilities.

I had my ups and downs with FAI Honorary Treasurer Joe Delaney – and there were probably more downs than ups. On the eve of the official party's departure for the 1994 World Cup finals, Ireland played a friendly against the Czech Republic before a packed Lansdowne Road. The Czechs triumphed 3–1, but the result wasn't of any great significance. Even Jack regarded this game as a chance to say 'thank you' to all the Irish fans who were unable to travel to the US to support the team.

After halftime, Jack invited me to join him, Maurice Setters, Mick Byrne, Charlie O'Leary and the substitutes in the dugout. Midway through the second half, one of the security men approached me and told me that Joe Delaney wanted to speak to me under the West Stand. Joe read me the riot act, and told me that he, rather than Jack, was the boss and that I was never to go near the field of play again. A few minutes after the final whistle, Jack got wind of what had happened – not from me, I might add – and they enjoyed a verbal set-to, during which Jack informed Joe that there was only one boss of the football team and that wasn't Joe.

Thankfully, the matter was patched up and Joe and I enjoyed a working relationship during the World Cup finals. For instance, a week before the tournament began, Jack and I travelled down to Miami from Orlando to watch Mexico, our second opponents in our group, play Northern Ireland in a friendly. Joe was delighted that I was able to accompany Jack on the journey, and we worked as a team in accessing as much information about the Mexicans as possible. We saw enough that afternoon to realise that they were no slouches, and so it proved as they beat us 2–1 under the horrendous midday sun of the Citrus Bowl in Orlando.

Jack's uncanny way of sensing trouble was never so clearly illustrated as on that trip to Miami when he voiced concerns to me that all was not well back at base in the North Orlando Hilton Hotel. When Jack walked back into the hotel, Maurice Setters informed him that there had been a minor players' revolt because Maurice had asked the players to run a few extra circuits of the training ground. The temperature that day had been even higher than normal, and Maurice's request prompted an angry exchange with Andy Townsend, who was voicing a collective feeling of frustration.

Roy Keane had been singled out by the media as the leader of this 'mutiny', but it was definitely Andy. The following day, Jack paraded Roy in front of a press conference, where Roy truthfully replied that he had not argued with Setters.

Life is rarely dull when Jack is around. I have been privileged to watch the great man in action. More than that, I have been able to get to know the man behind the image, and he is even more impressive. Jack and I are still in regular contact. Last July, my girlfriend, Melanie, and I enjoyed a few relaxing days down in Ballina with Jack and Pat. I even managed to catch a tasty salmon in the River Moy, a place where Jack is arguably at his most content. It's 13 years since I first introduced myself to Jack Charlton in the arrivals lounge of Logan airport in Boston. Those years have been full of great memories, and I know there are plenty more to come.

9

THE GRACES

IF ever a man was meant to be born on 1 April, it's Brendan Grace. Brendan is one of Ireland's funniest entertainers, and has kept people in all four corners of the earth in stitches for more than three decades. A comedian who can compare with the best in any sphere of show business, Brendan is living proof that quality never goes out of fashion. As a teenager, I was left with bellyache any time Brendan's character Bottler appeared on RTÉ television or radio. A true professional at his job as actor and comedian, Brendan is probably as popular now as he ever was. How many entertainers who started out in the same era as him can truly claim that?

I have seen Brendan in concert many times, and he would always have the audience eating out of his hand. Later on, I booked him for gigs in the Blackthorn. A Brendan Grace gig in the Blackthorn is always special. There's never any doubt that the chirpy, larger-than-life Brendan will pack them in. That's a feat he repeats through the US, Ireland, Britain and Australia.

Brendan works so hard and I often wonder how he keeps going at such a pace. A few years back, Brendan's daughter, Melanie, and myself were with him at a gig in Donegal. He was supposed to spend the night there but drove home to Dublin. Melanie and myself stayed in the hotel as arranged. The next morning, Brendan rang us from his mobile to tell us that he was already on his way to Killarney for another show. Even when he's relaxing in his holiday home in Florida, Brendan finds it hard to sit still. It usually gets to the stage when his wife, Eileen, has to hide his mobile to make him relax.

One of the main reasons Brendan remains so popular is the fact that he refuses to use bad language in his shows, unlike so many of his contemporaries. Two generations have grown up laughing at Brendan. Now a third is coming through, because parents can bring their kids to the shows. When he does summer shows at the Gleneagle Hotel in Killarney, he brings the youngsters up to the front and makes them feel important. I think this ability to connect with children makes him special.

Some comedians, singers, actors and musicians find it hard to survive outside their own sphere of entertainment, but such problems have never hindered Brendan. I've seen him receive reverential treatment from people of all backgrounds. Only a few years ago, Larry Mullen of U2 myself, Brendan and a few friends back to the band's hotel after their Elevation Tour date in Boston. When the Edge spotted Brendan, he marched straight over to him and blurted out 'Free a nipper' – which was one of Brendan's catchphrases from the 1970s television advert for Maxol petrol.

Another of Brendan's creations from that era was the great Bottler who had us all in stitches with his hard 'chaw' antics. Brendan even drove down to collect Melanie from school dressed as Bottler, which would drive her mad with mortification.

No matter how much time he spends on the stage or on television, there's no escaping the fact that Brendan is a true family man. Nothing gives him more pleasure and satisfaction than spending time with his wife, Eileen, and children, Melanie, Amanda, Bradley and Brendan – or Brendan Patrick as we call him.

We've all heard tales of former show business legends falling on hard times for one reason or another. Genuine hard luck stories abound, but there are frequent occasions when the cause of a once household name's exit from the limelight is self-inflicted. In such cases, it can sometimes be hard to sympathise if he or she has drunk the entire proceeds of a successful career.

Brendan was never going to squander his earnings, and he always maintained that providing a good home for his family was his first aim. He likes nothing more than to get into the kitchen and to cook a meal for everybody. There's a great story about Brendan's love of his grub while he was on tour with Paddy Reilly in Australia. One evening before a concert, an exiled Irishwoman took it upon herself to prepare a traditional Irish dinner of spuds, steak and all sorts of vegetables in the kitchen at the venue. Brendan's eyes were popping out of his head as he watched the meal being assembled.

When they had eaten the meal, Brendan went out of his way to compliment the woman for her efforts and admitted that he missed home cooking when on the road. With that, the woman invited Paddy and Brendan up to her family home for Sunday lunch. Delighted with the invitation, the two boys headed into the concert in tremendous form. On the Sunday morning in question, they met in the hotel bar for a few gin and tonics before heading off for lunch.

A taxi was ordered and off they set for their full Irish dinner. 'Where are we going?' said Brendan to Paddy.

'What do you mean? You've got the address,' replied Paddy.

'Aw, for f***'s sake, Paddy, what are you after doing?' Brendan cried.

They soon realised that neither of them had bothered to get the woman's address. Despite a series of phone calls, they were unable to discover where she lived. A few months later, Brendan eventually tracked down her address and wrote her an apologetic letter explaining what had happened. She wrote back admitting that she had cried when she read Brendan's explanation, as she had thought they had forgotten all about her.

Brendan's blessed with a tremendous manner and can raise a laugh from the most innocent incident or throwaway remark. There's always a reason to smile when he's around. He has this little saying: 'That should be grand but I'm going to have to run it by the handbrake.' Like many's the man before him, Brendan knows that it's always best to get the approval of the other half before embarking upon any mission. I'm sure he'll shoot me for letting that secret phrase out of the bag!

Down through the years, Brendan has always been very good to me, playing a few gigs in the Blackthorn every year. On one of his visits to us, Boston was basking in a heatwave, with the temperature hitting 85 degrees. Our air conditioning broke down, but Brendan made sure the show went on even though he lost about 10 pounds in the process! It's no wonder that he's so thin these days – he lost most of his weight in the Blackthorn that night!

Brendan gives a lot of his time to charity. He's heavily involved in the Bubblegum Club, which looks after terminally ill children, and is a fantastic supporter of Our Lady's Hospital for Sick Children in Dublin, where he frequently calls in unannounced to visit the kids and their families, as well as the nurses and doctors. When my late father, the Colonel, was in hospital in Mullingar, Brendan would nip in for a quick visit if he was in the vicinity. And if he couldn't drop in, Brendan would send him a bottle of whiskey, which was the Colonel's favourite.

On more than one occasion, I've been with Brendan when a person approached him and thanked him for sending his granny or mother a videotape of one of his concerts. That will have stemmed from a conversation six months earlier in a pub or restaurant, when Brendan took down the person's address and promised to send them a tape. Tommy Lowry, a friend of mine from Castletowngeoghegan, once told Brendan that his father was a big fan. Within a week, Brendan's new video was dropping through the letterbox.

Patience is a virtue that all entertainers must have. One night, Brendan and myself were enjoying a jar in Dublin when a fella, who was half cut, came over to annoy us. 'You're a great man going

round the place codding all the people and making loads of money,'
he informed Brendan. 'You're making a fortune from just making
people laugh.' Well, in my book anybody who gets up on a stage
and makes people laugh is a saint. Brendan was well able for this
halfwit. 'Oh yeah, Texaco fill my car with free petrol, Michelin put
tyres on the car for nothing and hotels never charge me for staying
a night with them,' said Brendan, as your man slunk away.

It's not only Brendan that makes the Grace family what it is:
Eileen is one in a million. A tremendous wife and mother, Eileen
is blessed with an amazing ability to organise. Eileen's parties are
fantastic, and I often wonder how she has the patience to do it.

My first introduction to Melanie came via my late, great friend
Tommy McGann, when he had Brendan Grace over to do a couple
of gigs in his bar in 1998. I went to the gig, met Brendan and agreed
to link up with him for a drink the following day. That day, Brendan
told me his daughter, Melanie, had secured a scholarship to
Emerson College in Boston. Emerson is famous for its drama
school; a lot of big names in Hollywood have come through it.
Brendan had secured an apartment for Melanie, but there was
nowhere for her to park her car. He asked me whether I knew of
anywhere.

'She can park the car at my house and any time she wants it, she
can just get down on the train and pick it up,' I told him. Melanie
arrived in Boston shortly afterwards. She left her car at my house
and introduced herself and her boyfriend to me. She often came to
the Blackthorn with her friends from college, and I would throw
them a couple of free beers. We became great friends, but never in
my wildest dreams did I think that we'd hook up. I knew her for a
few months coming and going, and became very fond of her.

In September 1998, Tommy McGann tragically died in a car
accident. The following St Patrick's Day, the city of Boston named
a street in Boston after him and held a remembrance day for him.
It was a big occasion for the Boston Irish. Myself and Pete Nash,

another Boston publican, went down to pay our respects to Tommy that day. Several drinks ensued, so we headed back to the Blackthorn. Melanie was there with all her friends. And as my mother used to say 'what you said quietly sober comes out drunk'. I obviously said something very nice to her that day because we sparked something off. All I remember is lying in the bed the next morning with a sick head, when I got a phone call from Melanie. 'Do you remember what you said to me last night?' she asked, to which I replied 'Well, now, what was that?'

'You better put your thinking hat on,' she said, adding, 'do you want to do lunch today?' I met her in the 'Littlest Bar in Boston', where we had a few beers. That was the start of our romance.

Soon after, we went to New York for a weekend. She told her parents that she was going to a do with Frank Gillespie's Gaelic footballers. I think they were starting to smell a rat. Melanie went down to see her parents in Boston, where Brendan was celebrating his birthday, and her parents were renewing their marriage vows on their 25th wedding anniversary. The three of them were out having a drink, when Brendan asked Melanie, 'How is Frank?'

She replied, 'Frank is great, Dad.'

'Aw, that's good. Well, you tell him I was asking for him.'

Melanie then confirmed what Brendan and Eileen were probably well aware of. 'I'm very fond of Frank,' she said.

'Aw, yeah,' added Brendan. 'Sure, Frank looks after everybody when they go to Boston.'

'Yes, Dad, but I'm very fond of Frank,' she continued.

Brendan looked Melanie straight in the eye in the way that only a father can and said, smiling: 'Frank Gillespie is too old to be my son-in-law.' So the ice was kind of broken.

My biggest fear was Brendan and Eileen's reaction to the age difference. I was then in my early forties and Melanie was in her early twenties. Shortly afterwards, I met Brendan for a pint in the Blackthorn. He assured me that he had no problem with the relationship, as long as I treated Melanie well. But I had to get by the war office, and the war office was Eileen. Unfortunately, I didn't meet Eileen until after the serious car accident Melanie and I were involved in, in May of 1999. I now count myself lucky to be regarded as part of the Grace family. These days, Melanie and I spend a lot of time with Brendan and Eileen in their house in Killaloe, County Clare.

Like Brendan, Melanie was born with a fantastic sense of humour and also does her share of stand-up comedy. I think that takes real guts. I admire her so much when she stands up in front of a crowd who may be well tanked up with booze. Melanie's career is moving in the right direction, although attending casting sessions is often far from glamorous.

Away from that end of the cutthroat business, Melanie holds drama classes for kids in Dublin and Killaloe when she is in Ireland. It requires a lot of talent to hold youngsters' attention and help them develop their own talents. A few months back, I went along with Melanie to a play staged by a children's group in Ballymun to mark the start of the demolition of the blocks of flats. Melanie had worked with the children. It made me very proud to think that my girlfriend had helped these kids – some of whom came from very tough backgrounds – to show their ability on the stage. The kids were first class.

I know that Melanie has the ability and drive to carve out a successful career in entertainment. She's the first to admit that it's not going to be easy, but she's really determined. In the last five and a half years, Melanie has taught me so much about life, and I know that the two of us still have much to experience. And if we're ever looking for a word of advice, then we know the perfect place to get it – her father.

10

A Keane Edge

THE Irish have always treasured our sporting heroes, be they on the home fields where Gaelic football and hurling are played out with such passion, or on the international stage when the green shirt has bestowed glory on Irishmen and women.

Over the past 15 years, we've witnessed one of the most remarkable Irish sporting careers: Roy Keane's progression from budding teenage star with Cobh Ramblers in the League of Ireland First Division to international superstar in the colours of Ireland and Manchester United. I'm old enough to remember George Best weaving his magic for the Old Trafford club and Northern Ireland. For the Republic of Ireland, Johnny Giles, Liam Brady and Paul McGrath earned the same level of respect from their peers and fans.

But Roy has always been that bit different, because his exploits for Ireland have often sparked controversy amongst the fans. And that was even before the incredible events in Saipan in May 2002. Like everybody else who followed those amazing few days in Saipan, I was left spellbound by the drama and fervently hoped that the problems between Roy and manager Mick McCarthy could be ironed out before the opening group game against Cameroon. But knowing both men as I do, it did not greatly surprise me that Roy watched the finals from his home in Manchester.

I've known Roy for more than 12 years, and regard him as a friend. As such, I can state with some degree of authority that he's smarter, warmer and more level-headed, than he's given credit for. Yes, he's fiery and temperamental, but that is because of his 100 per cent commitment to Ireland and United.

I first met Roy during the Irish team's trip to the US Cup '92, but we got to know each other a lot better when I started travelling over to Dublin for games in the years that followed. We would meet up after matches in Lansdowne Road at the official FAI-Opel players' receptions. After Ireland defeated Latvia 4–0 at Lansdowne Road in September 1992, I went back to the team hotel for a few pints with Roy, his brothers, Johnson, Denis and Pat, and parents, Mossie and Marie. Roy threw a plastic bag over to me, containing his match jersey. That was the first of the many match shirts he gave me.

Roy has always been a big fan of the Blackthorn and likes the craic that goes on in the place. If he could squeeze in a trip to Boston during the summer, he looked upon it as an opportunity to relax.

In June 1993, I made the week-long trip to the newly independent Baltic states of Latvia and Lithuania, where the Ireland team was playing two crucial World Cup qualifiers. After my success in organising the post-match social activities during US Cup '92, I was asked to scout out places for the lads to go for a drink after Ireland games. Roy would always approach me, and say, 'Frank, make sure you get a good place for a pint after the game'. It was hard work, but I suppose somebody had to do it! I'd go around two or three different joints. I either got a slagging if it was no good or received plenty of praise if it was up to scratch.

After the victory over Latvia in Riga, we were walking briskly towards the bar I had looked at earlier in the day. It was cold, so Roy took off his jacket, which was one of the FAI's official Opel jackets for players, and gave it to me. 'Now, Frank, make sure you give me that jacket back at the end of the night. Don't let anything happen to it,' he said.

That night, Steve Staunton and myself ended up going all over the beautiful old city. We met this fella whom we reckoned was in the local mafia, and he chauffeured us around in his brand new BMW. There were times when Stan and I were getting a bit scared. This fella wanted to buy Roy's jacket from me! No matter where he brought us, he kept saying to me, 'The jacket, the jacket, how much?' When he opened his wallet, he had more money than I had ever seen in one man's fist. At the end of the night, he offered me something like $350 for the jacket, which was only worth about $50. I was very tempted, but I was determined to give the jacket back to Roy. The next morning, I told Roy what had happened, expecting him to praise my loyalty. 'Frank, you must be mad. Why didn't you sell it to him and give me half?' he quipped.

The more I got to know Roy, the greater was the rapport between us. Our friendship was not hindered by his €5.5m transfer from Nottingham Forest to Manchester United in July 1993. In fact, I would probably say that he grew to appreciate our relationship even more as his profile grew in the English game. He knew he could fly out to Boston to escape the pressures of life at Old Trafford.

Roy even discussed his wedding plans to his girlfriend Theresa with me before he told his own dad. In May 1997, Roy bought a house for his mother and father just outside Cork. They had arranged a housewarming party, to which I was invited. On the night before the party, Ireland had crushed Liechtenstein 5–0 in a World Cup qualifier at Lansdowne Road. Roy and I were flying down to Cork the next morning. I insisted on heading back to stay the night in my house in Lucan (where I was living while managing the Dublin Baggot) and to pack a few clothes, much to the disagreement of Roy who insisted that 'they sold clothes in Cork, too'.

When I got back to the team hotel the next morning, I asked Mick Byrne whether he had called Roy. 'Roy never went to bed,' stated Mick. After Roy emerged from the bar, we headed off on the eight o'clock flight to Cork. Roy and myself were sitting together; most of the other passengers seemed to be Americans. I'm sure they thought it was very peculiar for these two fellows to be singing the 'Boston Burglar' at that hour.

As we flew south, Roy turned to me and informed me that he had something to tell me. Although I knew that I would not tell a soul, I immediately told him not to reveal this piece of information, as I did not want to be blamed for it leaking out. 'No Frank, I trust you. I'm not even telling Mossie this until the morning in question,' he said, adding, 'I'm getting married to Theresa next week and you're invited.' I was gobsmacked on two counts. One, that he was telling me such an important piece of information and, two, that I was on the list of guests at what was to be such a small gathering. Unfortunately, I couldn't go to the wedding, as I had a crucial business matter to attend to back in Boston.

We arrived in Cork shortly afterwards and were picked up by Theresa. But just before we linked up with her, Roy whisked me over to see Jack Charlton's statue in the terminal building. The sculpture shows Jack sitting down fishing, and Roy got a great kick out of it.

Marie, of course, had a big fry ready for us when we reached the house, and then we went to bed for a few hours. When we surfaced in the afternoon, I saw Roy with his daughters, Caragh and Shannon. He is devoted to his kids. Roy and Theresa later had two more children, Aidan and Leah.

Going to Cork with Roy always meant the warmest of welcomes from Mossie, Marie and the family and a hell of a session with some, or all, of the Keane family. The following afternoon, I set off for Mossie's local, the Templeacre, in the company of Mossie, Roy and his brothers, Johnson, Denis and Pat.

We sat down for our first pint at about half past three, and it didn't take long for a bit of a singsong to start. I became master of ceremonies. I split the bar into two halves and said, 'You fellas over there are Liverpool, and us lads here are Manchester United. We'll keep the singsong going to make a match out of it, and there might be a prize afterwards for the winners.'

By this stage, people were ringing their friends, mothers, brothers, sisters, girlfriends and anybody else they could think of, telling them to get up to the Templeacre as fast as possible in order to take part in this singsong. We kept it going for about two hours, with the banter from each side increasing the level of competition by the minute. Being an impartial MC, I had Liverpool up by three goals coming to the last song. But it was Mossie's turn to sing, so I knew that all was not lost for the United boys, as he has a superb voice!

Mossie's song was greeted by a massive round of applause. 'For that great song I have to give Mossie Keane a hat trick,' I said. 'And those three goals leave it all level.' At that point, I thought I was going to get a hiding from the Liverpool section. I quickly calmed it all down when I said, 'Relax, lads, because Roy is going to buy a drink for the house.' Roy stared at me, 'Frank, I never said that'. I shouted back, 'Get to the bar and after you've finished that one, lads, I'll buy you one myself.' Everyone had such a great time that the next day the owners of the Templeacre rang the Keane house asking for me to go up.

***

Being in the company of Roy gave me a great insight into how simply he approaches his life. He may live in a massive house and drive a flashy car, but he does not seek the limelight. Despite Roy's best efforts, there were times when he could not avoid trouble. On one particular visit to Cork, Roy and I enjoyed a few drinks in the Templeacre before going to a nightclub in town. We were only in the door a few minutes, when this fella had a go at Roy. Your man put his hand in the breast pocket of Roy's shirt and ripped it.

Needless to say, there was a little set-to and we headed back to Roy's parents' house.

When we got back, Mossie and Marie were enjoying a drink with a few neighbours. I warned Roy to go upstairs and change his shirt before he saw his folks. However, Roy went straight into the sitting-room and sat down. Marie looked at him and blessed herself, while Mossie rubbed his head. 'What's wrong, Roy, what happened?' asked Marie.

'Ah, just some assholes,' Roy replied. 'You know how it is. I can't go anywhere.'

Marie was slightly concerned, but Mossie saw fit to crack a joke: 'Roy Keane, it's times like this I wish to f*** you were a small farmer.'

On another occasion in the Baggot Inn in Dublin, the management decided to host a low-key get-together for the Ireland team. The Fureys provided the entertainment, and we had a great night. As the boys were leaving, a fella on the street began to give them a bit of a slagging. He actually spat at Roy. If I remember correctly, the idiot in question was a Leeds United fan, who drunkenly started shouting that Manchester United were scum. To his credit, Roy more or less laughed if off. Of course, this fella was probably down in the pub a few weeks later cheering for Ireland and Roy.

Not too long after that unnecessary confrontation in Baggot Street, Roy, Denis Irwin, Kevin Moran and myself ended up in the Dublin nightclub Lillie's Bordello. My son, Trevor, was with us and was having his first legal drink, after just turning 18. Roy and Trevor, whom Roy has known since he was a kid, were talking at the bar. A girl came over to them, excused herself and asked Roy for his autograph. Being his customary polite self, Roy scribbled out the autograph. As he handed the piece of paper to her, she asked whether she could give him a kiss. Roy turned his cheek and she gave him a little peck. The girl's boyfriend got jealous and started to shout over at Roy and give him 'the finger'. The gombeen walked over to us and spat at Roy. This time, Roy saw red and dived at him. Luckily enough, Trevor held him back. We called the bouncers, who threw the idiot out.

The following morning, I met Roy and he said: 'Tell your son, Trevor, thanks very much for last night. That's what I have to put up with, you know?' It actually got to the point that Roy has stopped going out to certain places. As a result, he would travel over to Dublin for games and spend his time in the hotel room.

Roy has mellowed with age. On the most recent occasion I saw him hassled by a wind-up merchant, he dealt with it very calmly. One evening, I bumped into Roy and Mick Byrne, and we all stopped for a few minutes and began to natter. About four or five fellas came over and asked Roy for his autograph, which he was more than happy to give them. One of them couldn't resist the chance to have a verbal dig at Roy and asked his mate, 'Who's he?'. He then addressed Roy, 'But I want your autograph anyway'. Roy looked straight through him, and replied, 'You should be on stage, boy'.

Roy looks set to go into football coaching and management, and there's no doubt in my mind that he would make a first class leader of men off the field, just as he's done so on it for the last 15 or so years. If Roy decides to move away from football or even retire from sport altogether, he's already earned enough money to look after his whole family. He has also used his wealth to help those people less fortunate than himself. I've seen Roy handing over cash and cheques to worthy causes. Many of these donations have never shown up in the media. That's the way Roy likes to do his business, so I'm not going to reveal the amounts involved or the recipients. Roy is also happy to buy everybody in his company a drink, as he did for about 70 of my regulars on the night that Ireland lost 2–0 to Holland in the 1994 World Cup finals in Orlando.

Roy is a person who will take a stance on an issue that affects him personally or a larger number of people. Maybe we should all have seen Saipan looming after his intervention on a number of issues at Old Trafford during the 1990s. When I go to see Manchester United play at Old Trafford these days, I am always aware of the difference in the players' lounge. Back in the mid-1990s, an unbelievable number of people would corner Roy in the lounge to ask for autographs. Roy got that stopped and ensured that only family members and close friends were allowed into the lounge. Roy was then instrumental in getting a crèche built for families going to the games.

It was in the players' lounge that I bumped into Posh Spice for the one and only time, though at the time I had no idea who she was! After a match, I was waiting for Roy and Denis to join me in the lounge. I sat down beside a girl and she began to talk away to me, asking me where I was from and if I was related to the lads. Denis then walked in and I went over to him.

'Frank, where are you sitting?' he asked.

'I was sitting there, talking to that girl,' I replied.

'Do you know who that is?' he said, to which I shrugged my shoulders. 'That's Posh Spice.'

Roy then came into the room and was told the story by Denis: 'Frank was sitting down talking to Beckham's woman.' Roy chuckled and said, 'Frank, you're an awful man, Posh is three months pregnant'.

There's no doubt that Roy's serious cruciate ligament operation in the autumn of 1997 and his marriage to Theresa a few months earlier helped him to adopt a more mature attitude to life. I'm also sure that Manchester United's insistence on players keeping in the right shape for the modern game was an influence. You cannot go out three and four nights a week and expect to match the new super-fit players who operate in the Premiership and Champions League. It's been a good thing for Roy that he did step back, as he's probably an even better player now.

I think Roy had reached the stage where all the hero worship may have been tiring him out. While Paul McGrath, Kevin Moran and John Aldridge were all given the VIP treatment in public, I never saw any player provoke the same reaction as Roy. One particular night, myself and most of the Irish squad were in a club in Malahide. I was standing beside Roy, and it was incredible the number of people who wanted to say hello to him. They scarcely bothered the rest of the lads. Roy got a bit frustrated, as he couldn't even enjoy his pint. 'Frank, is there a back door out of here?' he asked me. We ended up going out an emergency door, climbing a back wall and nearly getting our arses eaten off when a dog jumped at us.

**

While becoming friendly with Roy over the years, I have had the added bonus of getting to know his parents, Mossie and Marie. The hospitality they have shown me in Cork has always been fantastic, so I was thrilled when I was able to offer some in return. One day, Roy rang me and told me that he was thinking of sending his mam and dad over to Boston for their 37th wedding anniversary. 'Would you look after them and get them a nice hotel?' he enquired.

'No problem,' I replied, 'but I'm not going to get them a hotel because I've loads of room here in my place.' Roy was delighted.

'Mam will just want to shop, while Dad will just want to go to the pub,' he advised me. We had a great time with them, rounding off the celebrations with a big party in the Boston Baggot.

Roy rang every second day to see how the holiday was going. One morning, I was outlining to Mossie a trip down to Cape Cod to see a number of historical monuments and graves of the Kennedys. 'How far away is that?' asked Mossie. 'Ah, it's about two hours,' I replied. I could see that he wasn't too happy about the prospect of the trip. When the phone rang with Roy on the other end, I put Mossie on to him. Mossie took his chance: 'Roy, will you have a chat with Frank, as I think he's losing it. He wants to bring me down to the Cape, which is two hours away, to see auld monuments, tombstones and dead people, when I could walk three minutes to a pub to speak to people who are alive!'

That summed up Mossie perfectly. He loves nothing better than a chance to sing a song or engage in banter with friends. He's a truly great character. He has had to put up with an awful lot of grief, because of people's jealousy at his son's success. People will bicker with Mossie in the pub, and there are even lads who tap him for cash.

Marie is a real lady. You'd never be hungry in the Keane house. One morning when I was down in Cork, Marie served me up four eggs, six rashers, black and white pudding, fried bread and a big mug of tea. Roy was down the road getting the papers. When he came back and saw the feed, he exclaimed, 'Mam, you're feeding Frank better than you're feeding me'.

My last trip down south was just after Roy returned to the Ireland set up for the friendly victory over Romania at Lansdowne Road in May 2004. The entire Keane family are immensely proud of Roy's decision to resume his international career, as am I.

11

THE BOYS IN GREEN

FROM the late 1980s, Ireland has been a force to be reckoned with on the football stage. The team has had brilliant managers in Jack Charlton and Mick McCarthy, great players in Paul McGrath and Roy Keane and the best supporters on the planet. All this has helped the team to qualify for three World Cup finals and one European Championship. Yet, if you were to ask me to pinpoint another reason for the team's success, the first name off my tongue would Mick Byrne, a sports fanatic from the south inner city of Dublin.

Mick was the Ireland team physiotherapist from the Johnny Giles' era of the 1970s until the arrival of Brian Kerr's broom in February 2003. Trusted by the managers he served and adored by the players he treated, Mick played a central role in the Ireland set up. Like many Ireland fans, I associated Mick with the backroom staff of Big Jack's side. It was only when I got really close to the players and management staff during the 1990s that I realised how crucial he was to the side's success. Mick is no ordinary physio – he's a psychologist, priest and father figure all rolled into one. He treated the players like they were his own sons.

In the early days of my association with the Irish squad, Mick welcomed me with open arms. If I arrived at the squad's Dublin base and there wasn't a hotel room available, Mick always let me stay in the kit room. Mick was happy that I was acting as the squad's unofficial social manager. 'You're always welcome to stay with us because I know where the lads are when you're with them,'

Mick said to me. If Jack imposed a curfew, Mick would hold me responsible for its implementation.

In many ways, Mick was one half of a famous double act – the other half being kit man Charlie O'Leary, a man well known in Irish football as a top League of Ireland referee, a very capable junior football official and a hardworking member of the backroom staff under Jack Charlton and then Mick McCarthy.

Mick's other great sporting passions are Gaelic games. In 1998, Mick became the physio for the Galway Gaelic football team. He often told me how proud he was of the part he played in the team's victory in the All Ireland final that year. Three days after that match, Mick and I went to Tuam for the All Ireland winners' traditional GOAL charity match against the Rest of Ireland Selection. That night in Tuam, I witnessed how the Galway players loved Mick and also the way he looked after them.

I had met the Galway manager John O'Mahoney before, so we sat down after the game and enjoyed a quiet pint together. John explained why he had brought Mick into the Galway set up. He knew that the arrival of such a well-respected sports physio would give the squad a timely boost during the Connaught championship. John wanted to give the players a bit of a surprise, so he opted not to tell them in advance. Mick walked into the dressing-room during the normal chat before a training session. John said he could see the hair standing up on some of the lads' heads. John openly admitted that he did not believe Galway would have lifted the Sam Maguire Cup that year without Mick Byrne.

Mick always gave 110 per cent to everything he did. He even worked his magic on the Wolfe Tones, the Gaelic football team I was involved with in Boston. Mick came over to Boston for a visit, which coincided with the team's appearance in the semifinal of the local championship. Mick came down to the training field one night and put the lads through their paces. Mick was going through our lads one by one, having a chat with them, while rubbing their muscles to ease any aches or pains they had picked up. There were three or four other teams from the area training there as well. As Mick was finishing, one of the lads from one of the other teams came over, and asked, 'Frank, would it be alright if Mick had a look at one or two of our lads as well?' By the end of the night, Mick was giving advice to every team in South Boston!

***

I was truly sorry that Mick was not asked to stay on when Brian Kerr took over as manager of Ireland. The manner of his departure from the Irish set up, after so many years of service, seemed unfair. Mick was invited out to lunch by the new regime and asked about the best way to approach Roy Keane. However, at the lunch Mick soon realised he was not part of Brian's plans, so Mick sensibly turned round and said, 'Well, if that's the case, you can approach Roy in your own way'. Had Mick been kept on, I fully believe that Roy would have returned to the squad at the first invitation from Brian.

I suppose that all new managers want to assert their authority when they take charge, and, in that respect, Brian was no different from Mick McCarthy or Big Jack. When Mick McCarthy took over from Jack in February 1996. I suddenly found that doors that were previously open to me within the squad set up were now half closed, if open at all. Mick and myself would later enjoy quite a good relationship but I must confess that the first months of his reign were not to my liking.

Four months into Mick's reign, the squad arrived in Boston for the US Cup '96 tournament. They were based in a plush hotel in Newton, quite a distance outside the city. I think Mick wanted to keep the lads away from Boston, or maybe away from the Blackthorn. I arrived out at the airport to greet them off the flight from Dublin, and then made the journey to the hotel. Mick said he was giving the lads a day off and that they could go wherever they wanted.

Before I left the hotel, Mick brought me aside. 'The lads love having you around,' he said. 'I know that, but from now on there are different rules. There won't be any trips to the players' rooms and no travelling on the squad bus. Jack's not the manager any more.' 'Fair enough, Mick,' I calmly replied, even though I was quite annoyed because he was very blunt about it. However, I swallowed the new rules and everything was fine. While Mick was in Boston, I even ended up bringing him to buy a set of golf clubs.

When I arrived back in the Blackthorn, all the lads were there. The younger members of the squad were anxious to discover what the older lads had been talking about. They all wanted to serve behind the bar. Mark Kennedy, Ian Harte, David Connolly, Alan Moore, Kenny Cunningham, Keith O'Neill and Curtis Fleming all took their turns at the pumps. The lads thoroughly enjoyed their short stay in Boston, even though they lost 2–1 to the US in Foxboro Stadium.

I continued to fly over to Dublin for games and watched the young guns take over the mantle from Paul McGrath, Ray Houghton, Andy Townsend, Packie Bonner and John Aldridge. However, I kept a certain distance from the set up, as I did not wish to step on Mick's toes.

That remained the case for more than two years until an unusual set of circumstances helped to thaw the ice between Mick and myself. Ireland had failed to qualify for the 1998 World Cup finals, but had made a very encouraging start to the Euro 2000 qualifiers with a 2–0 victory over Croatia at Lansdowne Road in September 1998. In mid-October 1998, the team was due to play Yugoslavia away in Belgrade on a Saturday and then take on Malta at Lansdowne Road a few days later. I came back to Ireland, planning to take in both matches. NATO was threatening to bomb Belgrade at any moment because of Yugoslavia's bloody military campaign in Kosovo. UEFA finally gave in to FAI and Irish government pressure and sensibly postponed the Belgrade game for a month.

As a result, the lads had more than a week to prepare for the Malta game. I drove down to the team's new base in the very pleasant surroundings of the Kilkea Castle Hotel in County Kildare. I met up with the lads, who were allowed to have a few drinks after word came through that the Yugoslavia match was off. Everybody was having a fantastic evening, and Mick was in great form himself. After dinner, he said to me, 'I want a word with you, Frank'. I immediately thought I was in trouble again. Mick brought me into a quiet corner: 'You know when I came in first I had to crack the whip a bit.'

'I understand, Mick, no hard feelings. You had to do what you had to do,' I replied.

Then he turned to the real point of our conversation. 'I know that you know more than I do about certain squad matters because the lads tell you things that I don't hear about,' he said. 'So, what's the consensus on my relationship with the lads? What do they think? Is there anyone saying anything about me?'

'No, Mick,' I said back to him. 'Everything is fine and if you keep going the way you are, then I think everything will be okay.'

Even if the players had been talking about him, I wouldn't have broken their confidence. I made sure to get in the old saying that 'all work and no play makes Jack a very dull boy', and added that I believed the reason Jack got so much out of the lads was because he allowed them to enjoy themselves.

Soon after, I was back at Kilkea Castle during another international week. As I was getting out of the car, Mick was coming outside to talk to the press. He walked past the waiting journalists and snappers, came over and put his arms around me. 'You're very welcome, and I'm delighted that you're here,' said Mick, who later invited me back on the team bus.

Despite our early problems, Mick and his family always received a great welcome in the Blackthorn. Shortly after he took over the Ireland post, he arrived in with his wife, Fiona, and children, en route to Florida. I sorted him out with a hotel and even got a limo to take him shopping. I brought him down to the Blackthorn for a few drinks, but I don't think he was too impressed and we didn't stay long. But overall, Mick had a good time in Boston. Chris and myself went everywhere with him and we never let him pay for anything. We brought the kids around and showed them all the sights.

***

The Irish team from the late 1980s and early 1990s was blessed with big characters. Ronnie Whelan, Kevin Moran, John Aldridge, Tony Cascarino, Paul McGrath and Denis Irwin were all major stars on the pitch and lit up social gatherings off it. After an international at Lansdowne, the boys would file into the Opel reception in the old Lansdowne pavilion, where they could meet family and friends. Then it was back to the team base at the Forte Posthouse before heading into town. Madigans was usually the first stop, and the Baggot Inn in Dublin was also a regular haunt when I co-owned it. Then it was another taxi ride across to Rumours in O'Connell Street, where Krish Naidoo was always a very generous host.

They were the old soldiers who played like demons for their country, but who could also live it up without allowing it to affect their performances on the pitch. Jack Charlton was delighted to see the lads enjoying a pint because he believed that it helped them to build team spirit on the pitch. There was always a magnificent sense of camaraderie amongst the players, which I don't think any other football team could have matched.

Kevin Moran is the salt of the earth. Kevin's always happy to source tickets for me, be they for Manchester United or any Premiership match. He's also a fantastic businessman, and I'm honoured to say that I've called on his experience on more than one occasion. The biggest kick I get from Kevin is when we're walking into or out of Old Trafford – and by the way, his walk has me trotting. He's still stopped by fellas who want his autograph or a photograph – and that's almost 20 years after he left the club. The respect he commands from United fans is unbelievable.

Kevin is a people's person. He is never arrogant or rude to anyone who wants a few minutes of his time. The only time I saw Kevin losing his cool was on that infamous night in Windsor Park in 1993, when Alan McLoughlin's equalising goal sent us to the 1994 World Cup finals. Kevin was injured for that game, so he sat with me and Jack's great mate, 'Big' Dave Hutton, in the main stand. Kevin received dog's abuse during the 90 minutes, with oranges being continually thrown at him. Kevin stood up and threw a few choice words back at the offenders, and finally a few RUC officers took action to stop the provocation. When Alan scored that equaliser, I jumped from my seat, oranges or no oranges! If ever a man deserved his 15 minutes of fame, then it was Alan, who had trudged all over Europe but rarely came off the bench.

I will always treasure Kevin's testimonial at Lansdowne Road in 1994, because Jack invited me on to the bench as his assistant as Maurice Setters was absent.

It was with Kevin that I bumped into former US president Bill Clinton just a few days before the 1999 Ryder Cup at Brookline near Boston. Kevin was bringing a group of clients from the United Kingdom over for the famous golf showdown between the US and Europe, and he took a trip over to Boston prior to the event to ensure that the arrangements were in place.

I linked up with Kevin after his work was finished. We decided to play a round of golf at the Farmer's Neck course on Martha's Vineyard, close to where President Clinton – who was in the final months of his term in the White House – spent his annual holidays. On arrival, we learned that Bill was golfing that day, so it was little surprise that we were given a thorough frisking by his bodyguards before we set off for the first tee.

About 15 minutes later, Bill arrived out for his game. I voted Democrat and held the President in the highest esteem for his work on the Northern Ireland peace process, so I could not ignore this chance. The bould Kevin and myself seized the opportunity to introduce ourselves.

When Bill heard our brogues, he stopped and said with a smile: 'You guys must know my friend Bono.' He came over and shook our hands, before regaling us with tales of the U2 frontman. He spent a good 10 minutes with us, his arms around us as he explained his hopes for the peace process. 'Fingers crossed, lads, that my successor works equally as hard at it,' he said. President Clinton also expressed his gratitude to Taoiseach Bertie Ahern for his tireless work on the peace process. I often bumped into Bertie at Old Trafford. The next time I saw Bertie, I told him of the President's praise.

Aldo is probably the funniest man I've ever met. He can have you doubled in two with his wicked Scouse sense of humour. I've been a guest at his and Joan's home and really felt part of the family.

Ronnie – who played in the magnificent Liverpool side that won league championships almost at will in the 1980s and lifted the European Cup in 1984 – is a real gem. On the night after Ireland lost 2–0 to Holland in Orlando in the 1994 World Cup, Ronnie and myself were drowning our sorrows in a bar. Despite the result, the mood was positive as there was a general feeling that the team would bounce back during the next qualifiers.

Some joker then decided to let off a few bangers beside Ronnie and myself. It was funny the first time, but when it happened again and Ronnie was hit with a few sparks, we felt it was time to call a halt. Unfortunately, the 'clown' insisted on confronting Ronnie and was about to get physical, until a well directed left hook from your's truly sent him flying over an armchair! 'I never saw a man disappear so fast,' laughed Ronnie, as I revealed that I had been a keen amateur boxer during my schooldays in Tyrrellspass.

Paul McGrath's stature in Ireland was simply incredible. The public could not get enough of him. He was amazingly shy and that probably added to his allure. It's a pity that he took refuge in drink to the extent that he did. I found him to be one of the softest and most genuine people I have ever met. One night, Paul and myself visited Clontarf Castle in Dublin to see Paddy Reilly in concert. I was driving, and I would have had one or two pints on me, as we made our way back to the Forte Crest Hotel at Dublin airport. As we neared our destination, I heard a siren behind me. The Guards waved me over and I pulled down the window.

'Is everything okay, Guard?' I asked.

'Everything is fine but you have a flat wheel,' came the reply.

I had sensed a slight noise in the car, but I thought it was the bumpy road. When the Guards saw Paul in the passenger seat, they said 'Ah, it's yourself' and insisted on shaking his hand before changing the wheel for me.

Another lovely, unassuming man was Monsignor Liam Boyle. The Monsignor travelled extensively with the squad for many years and was instrumental in setting up the famous meeting between Jack's party and Pope John Paul II in Rome during Italia '90. Jack had a lot of time for Monsignor Boyle and would encourage the lads to attend the traditional pre-match mass. On several occasions, I served Communion at the mass for him. The Monsignor got on well with the players, and he wasn't afraid to muck in and carry the kit on and off the bus.

When the new Major League Soccer was established in the US in 1996, Frank Stapleton was appointed the first manager of the Boston Revolution football team. I was involved to a degree in the recruitment process for the team, as I was great friends with Corkman Brian O'Donovan, who was general manager of the Revolution.

I used to go to the odd game in the old soccer league, while Brian would come into me for a pint. It was on one such visit in the autumn of 1995 that he outlined his plan to sign a few Irish players for the Revolution. I arranged for him to fly to Lisbon in November of that year, so he could chat to the Ireland players before their Euro '96 qualifier against Portugal. Packie, Paul and John were just a few of the lads who spoke to Brian, as they were all at a late stage in their careers. However, the money wouldn't have been that fantastic as the salaries were all capped, and none of them took the plunge.

Soon afterwards, Frank got the job as manager. The Irish in Boston were all delighted, even if, at first, we couldn't believe that one of our own was going to manage the local soccer team. We couldn't wait for the first game. All the Irish bars in Boston got together and hired buses to go to the match at Foxboro Stadium. Each bar probably had two busloads of supporters.

We were all very disappointed that Frank did not come around to do a bit public relations work on behalf of the club, or to simply say 'hi' to us. The Irish in Boston are not silly and they could see that Frank was not trying to build up a relationship with them. Traditionally, the Irish back you in their droves if you make the effort with them. That was our first and last time to arrange buses to go to a Revolution match. I drove out to see them play a few other times, but there were few other takers for the trip.

Later, we found out that Frank did not get on with Alexi Lalas, who was the big star of the Revolution team. Lalas was pulling in the kids and the crowds. At that time, he was probably one of the top football attractions in the US. He always reminded me of Billy Connolly, because every time I saw him he was singing and playing the guitar, while sporting this mad, red beard. He was quite a character and I believe that the Revolution's owners, the Kraft family, wanted to play him all the time, which may not have sat well with Frank's views.

The only time I saw Frank afterwards was when he was sacked by the club. He came into the Blackthorn to present cups and medals to the local Bohemians football team that Chris and I had sponsored.

Denis Irwin was another great star for Ireland and Manchester United. I built up a great friendship with him over the years. If I opened my doors to Denis in Boston, then he did the same for me in Manchester. When United won their first Premiership title under Alex Ferguson in 1993, I was over in the city. Denis made sure that I was part of the official celebrations and was able to travel with the players, as the club paraded its first league crown since 1967.

A few days after they were crowned champions, the players went to Chester races at the Roodee. I went with them on the players' coach. My brother, John, who was watching the races on TV in his house in London, saw me sitting in the champagne bar quaffing as much of the stuff as I could get into me. The team skipper Bryan Robson told me that I was United's guest and need not buy a bottle of champagne. Then, Clayton Blackmore and myself won a couple of hundred quid on a 14–1 shot. It was that sort of day.

Denis and myself have continued to link up over the years, and I always enjoy chatting with him about football because he's one of the most knowledgeable men there is on that subject. And if you're looking for someone to sing 'The Fields of Athenry' or the 'Red Rose Café', Denis is your man. When we were in Orlando in 1994, Denis was carried from one end of Mulvaney's bar to the other, after a brilliant rendition of 'Willie McBride'.

For two lads who enjoy a laugh, Jason McAteer and Phil Babb probably top the table. As two-thirds of the 'Three Amigos' with Gary Kelly in 1994, the pair showed early promise for seeing the lighter side of life. Handsomely paid by Liverpool and enjoying life to the full as two eligible bachelors, Phil and Jason were regulars in the Blackthorn. You just never knew when they were going to drop in!

One afternoon, I had warned my barman, Peter Farrell, that I was not to be disturbed in the office, as I wanted to catch up with some paperwork. But ten minutes into the accounts and correspondence, Peter popped his head in the door to tell me that there were a few lads at the counter who insisted on seeing me. After giving Peter a piece of my mind, I reluctantly walked out into the bar to be greeted by the sight of Phil and Jason and two mates parked on stools and enjoying a drink called Zima. It transpired that they had hopped on a plane to Boston, armed only with their passports and toothbrushes in order to visit their pal Frank in the Blackthorn. They stayed for 10 days. I eventually got back to those bloody accounts, but only after a few dozen Zimas had been consumed.

12

BRUSH WITH DEATH

THERE are days in everybody's life that are forever etched into their memory. Births, marriages and deaths are the staple diet of life and are the defining moments of many people's existence. Then there are other events that go into the mental diary. They may be great sporting, artistic or political triumphs or just special private occasions. For myself and Melanie, Thursday, 13 May, 1999, is a date that will not readily slip from our minds. It was the day that we brushed with death.

One of my longest-serving and finest barmen, Peter Farrell, from County Meath was getting married to Ciara O'Leary down in Listowel in County Kerry. Although Melanie and I had only been going out with each other for a matter of weeks, we went home together to attend the wedding. We arrived home about a week before Peter and Ciara's big day, and took up an invitation from Matt Molloy of the Chieftains to visit him in Westport. We enjoyed a great night with Matt, and after lunch the following day we headed back for Tyrrellspass to have dinner with my sister, Claire. That night, we were due to stay at the Forte Crest Hotel at Dublin airport, ahead of our departure to Manchester to see United's last game of the season against Spurs at Old Trafford. Kevin Moran had organised tickets for us and was also bringing us along to a do that night. It was going to be a big weekend, as United needed to win the match to secure the Premiership title.

Melanie drove as far as Longford, where we got out to buy a few bars of chocolates and bottles of water. I decided that I'd drive the last leg from there to Tyrrellspass. By the time we reached Mullingar, it was rush hour. Melanie was tired and was lying back in the front passenger seat with her feet up. It was raining heavily, so the traffic was moving at a fairly slow pace in both directions. We were about two miles outside the town, when, suddenly, a car came out of nowhere. The driver tried to pass me out, even though there were cars coming towards us.

He tried to get back in on the left-hand side of the road by brushing against me. The impact knocked off my wing mirror and pushed me up on to the grass verge on the left-hand side of the road. Because of the downpour, the grass was so wet that the car slid along with the passenger wheels well down the bank. I was doing my utmost to stop the car, but it hit a gully, which pulled the steering wheel out of my hand and sent the car shooting across the road at about a 90-degree angle. I thought that this was the end for both of us.

Our car bounced off a Volvo truck that was thankfully almost stationary – the driver had slowed down when he saw us hurtling along the verge – and we ended up in the other ditch. Incredibly, I was not badly injured. I turned round to Melanie and all I could see was a cut on her head. I asked her if she was okay, genuinely believing that she was fine. I looked in the back of the car, and I could see the luggage coming in from the boot. I then said to Melanie: 'It's okay, don't panic, we're okay. We're still going to Manchester for the game.' It's funny how the mind works in these situations.

Any thoughts of football, league titles or anything connected with sport soon vanished when I heard Melanie's next words: 'My ankle, my ankle.' I looked down to see Melanie's ankle wrapped around the gear stick. I started to realise that this accident was far worse than it had first appeared. There was smoke everywhere, and my biggest fear was that the car was going to catch fire. I eventually got out my side, and fell couple of feet down the ditch. I couldn't get Melanie out of the car, as moving caused her too much pain.

As I staggered to the side of the road, I saw a fella coming towards me. 'Did you see that car?' I asked him. 'What the hell was going on? He was crazy passing out like that.' He replied that he had seen the car, and that he thought it was a D-registered white Audi. There were people coming from all directions to help us, including two doctors, Dr McMahon and Dr O'Donoghue, who gave Melanie a shot of morphine to kill her pain. The Mullingar fire brigade arrived quickly at the scene, and cut the roof off the car to reach Melanie. It took them an hour and a half to get her out, and that was probably the longest 90 minutes of my life.

Melanie was taken to Mullingar Hospital. Her father's manager, Brian Keane, arrived down from Dublin, and we phoned Brendan, who had just got off a flight from Ireland to New York. He turned around and got back on the same flight, to return to Ireland. The superb ambulance crew, doctors and nurses in Mullingar had done all that they could for Melanie, and were looking for a helicopter to take her to the Mater Hospital in Dublin. But it was a dark evening, and the only helicopters available were not built for night flying. Instead, Melanie was ferried to Dublin by an ambulance, which didn't go over 25 miles an hour. My brothers and sisters wanted me to stay the night in Mullingar Hospital, as I had a few broken ribs and cuts and bruises. I couldn't stay, though, as I was too concerned about Melanie. Brian then drove me to the Mater Hospital in Dublin.

The following morning, we learned the full and shocking extent of Melanie's injuries: two broken vertebrae, a broken leg, two broken knees and two broken ankles. It was a serious situation. I couldn't imagine how much pain Melanie was suffering. It was a very tough time for me, and must have been awful for Melanie's family, Brendan and Eileen, her sister, Amanda, and two brothers, Brendan and Bradley.

The next morning, Eileen arrived in from the States. Charles Haughey's son, Ciaran, flew us down to Shannon Airport by helicopter to pick her up and take her back to the Mater. That was the first time I met Eileen, and she was more than courteous to me. I would have understood if she had wanted to kill me at that moment. She was naturally very concerned about Melanie, particularly when the consultant, Frank McManus, informed us that Melanie had been so close to being paralysed. A sobering thought for us all, but one that must have truly frightened Melanie.

Melanie spent six weeks in intensive care and undergoing operations in the Mater. Through the grace of God, the attention of the nurses and the surgery carried out by Frank McManus, she made slow but steady progress. She was an unbelievable patient. While she was in the Mater, Mick McCarthy called in to visit her. 'If it was one of my lads with a broken finger they'd be lying, whinging in the bed,' said Mick. 'Melanie's plastered from head to toe, and she's in the bed playing the guitar!' Many of the Irish players visited her, including Phil Babb, Jason McAteer and Packie Bonner. And, of course, Mick Byrne went in to see her and cheer her up.

I had to go back to the States to sort out a couple of things, but I returned to be by Melanie's side, as she recuperated in the rehabilitation clinic in Clontarf in north Dublin. We spent the rest of the summer together, until she was ready to go back to college in Boston. With great determination, she hobbled back into the classroom on crutches, and because there were no elevators in the school she had to struggle up and down the stairs. Her fellow students really helped her out.

I was later charged with careless driving, but Justice Joseph Mangan dismissed the case in January 2001. Judge Mangan accepted that it was 'plausible' that the actions of the white car had caused the accident.

There's no doubt that the experience made me take stock of life. My biggest emotion was simply to thank God that Melanie had survived, because I don't know where I'd be today without her. I'm sure Melanie suffered her share of nightmares. We attended quite a few sessions of counselling at the time. We still talk to each other about that day and work on putting it to the back of our minds.

Melanie will probably never be physically the same again, but she refuses to dwell on it. She still has her aches and pains and always will, but I hope I'll be there to help her through the tough days.

***

Thankfully Melanie and myself can look back at that awful day in May 1999 and count our blessings that we survived. That's something that Tommy McGann, his family and large circle of friends cannot do. Little more than eight months before Melanie and I were in the accident, Tommy was tragically killed in a car crash while on a visit home to his native Kilmaley in County Clare.

Mention the name Tommy McGann in the Banner County or in Boston, and you won't hear a bad word said against him. The Irish often display a strange attitude to those who have passed on. The greatest walking b******* on earth can suddenly become a saint when laid six feet under, while I've heard terrible things muttered about decent men and women as the coffin was being lowered. With Tommy, it was all positive and every word was genuine. While he evolved from wheeler-dealer to successful businessman, Tommy always addressed the stockbroker and garbage collector as one and the same.

Tommy's unusual way of entering the States in the 1970s probably sums up the sort of character he was and his attitude to life. It's a story that was retold during the wake. Tommy was all but smuggled over to the States by a group of American policemen who were on holidays in Ireland! Tommy had been drinking with the policemen for several days, and they went for one final pint on their way to Shannon airport. The craic was so good that Tommy went with them to the airport. He ended up on the plane – no ticket, no passport, no money, no nothing. The plane touched down at Bradley airport in Connecticut, where just one part-time customs officer operated at that time.

Tommy sneaked through a side door and rang his mother back home: 'I won't be home for dinner!' I often asked him what his good mother said in reply. 'What could she say? Sure she knew I was wild!'

Spells in Springfield, Doolin and San Francisco followed before Tommy finally returned to Clare to set up what has become one of Ireland's most famous pubs, McGann's of Doolin. The pub was frequented by loads of musicians. Hence, the locals started the Doolin traditional music festival down there. Christy Moore wrote a song, called the 'Continental Céilí', which mentions the pub.

In the early 1980s, Tommy decided to try his luck back in the States. When he arrived in Boston, he initially worked in the Black Rose and Purple Shamrock pubs, but eventually bought a pub in Easton. He then opened the Irish Embassy in Cape Cod with his partner Joe Dunne from Dublin, and they later bought more pubs. They also set up a hostel, which catered for tourists and, importantly for Tommy, young Irish immigrants.

I first met Tommy in 1986, and we soon developed a close bond. One night, he told me, in his distinctive Clare accent, 'Sure, we're closer than brothers'. If any Irish person needed a piece of sound advice, then Tommy was the man they turned to. He was a great help when Chris and myself were buying the Blackthorn.

Tommy and I were both heading home to Ireland in autumn of 1998, and planned to meet up at Croke Park to watch the All Ireland football final between Galway and Kildare. Two weeks before the match, I spent a weekend in Cape Cod with the Fureys. We had a great night in Tommy's bar on the Cape. I stayed the night in Tommy's house, and the following morning he decided we'd go for a walk. I told him I had no gear for a walk, so he togged me out in a Carlsberg shirt, blue shorts and a pair of runners. 'Now you're a real Cape Codder,' he said. We walked about eight miles, with him constantly asking 'Are you getting tired?' I knew he was testing me. When the 'stroll' ended, I left Cape Cod and headed back to Boston, where I was to catch a flight to Ireland. I would never see Tommy alive again.

As I sipped a pint in the Blackthorn in Southie before departing for Logan airport, the phone rang with Tommy at the other end. 'There's a friend of ours, Matt Molloy, waiting for you at the airport,' said Tommy. I flew with Matt, exchanging stories about Tommy and our other friends. Matt told me that he was considering buying a boat in Canada, but it was a bit more expensive than he thought it was worth. Matt got off the flight at Shannon and I continued on to Dublin.

From there, I went to John Aldridge's 40th birthday bash in Liverpool. After the party, I stayed on in Merseyside for a few days, hanging out with Aldo, when he could spare the time from his job as manager of Tranmere Rovers. On the following Wednesday afternoon – 23 September – John and I were on our way to watch the second team play in the midlands. Aldo's car phone rang, and he picked it up. The call was for me. It was a mutual acquaintance of ours, Gary Omar.

'You have to ring Frank Smith in Dublin straight away,' said Gary. 'There's an urgent message there for you.'

'Gary, what is it? You have me shaking now, I'm not able to ring the number,' I asked.

'Aw, Frank,' he replied, 'I can't tell you.'

Naturally enough, everything went through my head. Had something happened to the kids or to... I wouldn't let Gary off the phone, and eventually he relented and told me that Tommy McGann had been killed in a road accident in Clare.

I dropped the phone on the floor of the car. I had to go to the game because it was Aldo's job. But Aldo gave me his mobile phone, so I could call anyone I wanted. After the game, he brought me straight to the airport and I got a flight to Dublin, and then flew on to Shannon. There was a wake that evening in the Usual Place bar in Ennis. The first people I met at the wake were Matt and Geraldine Molloy. As I put my arms round Matt, I said, 'Buy the boat'. Life is too short. I met Matt afterwards and he told me that he had taken my advice.

It was no surprise that thousands attended Tommy's funeral in Kilmaley, because he was so well respected. Finbar Furey, Seán Keane, Matt Molloy, Stockton's Wing, the Chieftains and numerous other musicians turned up to pay their respects. Tommy was divorced from his wife Kelly, who is magnificent mother to their son, Danny. Everybody's heart went out to young Danny and Tommy's girlfriend, Margaret Powers.

Like countless tens of thousands of others before him and since, Tommy arrived in the US aiming to work hard and build up a thriving business. But what marked him out as different was the fact that he gave so much back to the city and to other Irish men and women by fixing them up with a place to stay or a job. When the shock of Tommy's death finally passed, the good people of Boston and Clare went about organising their own special tributes to him. And what a response they got.

In Boston the following St Patrick's Day, a celebration of Tommy's life was held in Portland Street. The city's mayor, Tom Menino, Monsignor Francis Rossiter, Boston councillor at large Stephen J. Murphy, Gerry Dunleavey and Jim Farmer all spoke at the event. Boston City Council officially recognised Tommy's 'valuable contributions... to many people over his lifetime'. They voted to make 17 March, 1999, 'Thomas McGann day in the city of Boston'. That day, a street was re-named 'Tommy McGann Way', a fitting way to honour a man who gave so much to Boston and its people.

On 2 September, 1999, the citizens of Clare held the Tommy McGann memorial concert in Ennis' West County Inn hotel. The Saw Doctors, Ronnie Drew, Mike Hanrahan, the Clancys, Shaskeen, Kieran McDermott and many others played that night. It was a fitting tribute to a man who had showcased Irish groups and bands in his Boston pubs. I'm sure Tommy was smiling down from above when the proceeds from the concert were handed over to the charity foundation Tommy had set up in Boston. Money was also given to help build the impressive €325,000 Kilmaley Sports and Leisure complex in his home village.

Tommy and I classed ourselves as emigration brothers. Not many days of the week go by that I don't think of him. His passing at the age of 43 was all the more difficult to bear, as he had successfully battled a serious bout of cancer just a few years earlier. Tommy would have turned 50 next year, and I still find it hard to think that he will not be here to celebrate it with us.

***

The last few months have also been very tough for me. On Monday, 17 May, 2004, my father died at St Mary's Hospital and Nursing Home in Mullingar after a short illness at the age of 90.

Thankfully, I was in Ireland when my father took a turn for the worse a week before his death. I had spent a couple of months at home in Tyrrellspass and was due to fly back to Boston with Melanie on 15 May. But when the Colonel picked up a 'flu bug four days prior to our departure, I wisely opted to stay put. Over the weekend, the family became extremely concerned and the medical staff at the home prepared us for the worst.

But right to the end, the Colonel was in fine fettle, and even sang an old local song called 'Paddy Caherly' on the morning of his death. For me, that summed up his love of life and people. He had continued to keep the best side out, despite being confined to bed for several years. There was nothing he liked more than a drop of whiskey, and he always had a bottle of Power's in his bedside locker.

The Colonel's passing was peaceful and his children, grandchildren and great-grandchildren were present when he moved on from this world. The medical attention and support he received from all the staff at St Mary's for the previous six years was first class and something that was deeply appreciated by all his family.

The Colonel's wake and funeral in Tyrrellspass brought home many relatives and friends. Although we were all mourning the

Colonel's passing, being together gave us the opportunity to celebrate his full life.

***

The year 2004 also saw the untimely passing of Noel Maher – a great GAA fan from Tyrellspass – and Derek McCormack of the Barleycorn. It was also the year of the tragic death of one of Boston's most popular Irishmen, Dubliner Barry Mullally. Barry emigrated to the States in 1988 and worked with his brother Stuart in the city's construction business. He died as a result of the injuries he received in a fall from scaffolding on 15 March. Barry was kept on a life support system until St Patrick's Day, to give his heartbroken parents, Bertie and Kay, time to fly out from their Tallaght home to be by to his bedside.

Over the years, I've witnessed the outpouring of grief following the deaths of respected members of the Irish community in South Boston, but 36-year-old Barry's passing was even more moving. When the funeral hearse travelled down Broadway, around 2,000 people turned up to pay their respects to Barry. Two large cranes standing on either side of the street positioned their booms so that a tricolour could be hung above the passing cortege. In some small way, the support shown by the people of the area will hopefully have comforted Barry's widow, Louise, and his children, five-year-old Jack and Myia, who was three when the accident occurred.

Even in death, Barry showed what a great fella he was, because he was an organ donor card carrier. A 42-year-old Boston policeman – a married father of three – was given Barry's heart.

At times like this, the Irish community in Boston shows its real soul. The immigrants and Irish-Americans alike rallied around to raise funds for Louise and the children. I don't think that sense of community will ever change. When we win a football match we celebrate together, and when tragedy hits us we stick together.

13

MICHAEL FLATLEY HOLDS COURT

MENTION the name Michael Flatley to anybody of Irish descent in any corner of the world and you are almost sure to receive a flicker of recognition of his name. Scarcely has one person ever personified one form of entertainment as much as the Irish dancer from Chicago.

Michael starred with Jean Butler in Moya Doherty and John McColgan's ultra-successful Riverdance spectacular at the 1994 Eurovision Song Contest in Dublin. In recent times, he has starred in his own lavish dance productions. Many stars from the worlds of politics, sport, film and music have supped at the bar of the Blackthorn. However, I find it hard to pinpoint anyone who has made as big an impact in their chosen field as Michael has.

I first met Michael back in 1991, when he was one of the support acts on the Chieftains' US tour. One night, they all arrived in the Blackthorn. Michael may have been part of the Chieftains' entourage – one of Ireland's greatest-ever musical exports – but he was being paid a near pittance for the privilege of appearing on such a bill. I stood Michael a pint or two and we struck up an immediate rapport.

He told me how he had worked like a Trojan during his teens to perfect his skills both on the canvas of the boxing ring and on the floors of Chicago's Irish clubs, where Irish dancing was the currency of success. Michael informed me that he would achieve something big with his life. And after that initial meeting, I wasn't surprised that he made such a success of his life with Riverdance and the Lord of the Dance.

My first taste of Riverdance came in late 1994, when I attended a function in Dublin's Berkeley Court Hotel with Jack Charlton and his wife, Pat. Living in Boston I had missed the performance at the 1994 Eurovision Song Contest. After the dinner at the Berkeley Court, the Riverdance performance was played on a big screen. I was simply blown away.

Even then, Michael's thirst for success could not be quenched by Riverdance. When he created the idea of the Lord of the Dance, he wasn't afraid to break his ties with the Riverdance consortium and establish his own company. That sort of self-belief is a scarce but vital commodity in the world of show business. He went to the banks and successfully raised the millions needed to put Lord of the Dance on the road in the US and then all over the globe. That shrewd initial decision laid the foundations for an empire that now stretches all the way to a themed Irish hotel and entertainment complex in Las Vegas. During his phenomenal rise to success, I had not been in touch with Michael, probably because his demanding schedule didn't take him near Southie.

So, those few pints in the Blackthorn were our only contact until 16 June, 2002, when Ireland was playing Spain in the second round of the World Cup in the South Korean city of Suwon. My great mate Sean 'Spud' Murphy and myself had travelled from Seoul for the game, with Steve Staunton's father, Tom, and his brothers, David and Padraig. Steve had kindly arranged for us to travel on the players' families' coach. When we arrived at the stadium, somebody in the group told me that Michael Flatley had a seat in the other corner of the ground. Having not set eyes on Michael for 11 years, I decided to go over and say hello.

Michael was in the company of his then girlfriend, Lisa Murphy. Over I went, tapped him on the shoulder and waited for a reaction. 'Oh my God, Frank, the Blackthorn!' he cried, as he hugged and kissed me. He told everybody that I had served him Guinness in Boston back in the day when he didn't have the price of a pint.

We chatted for a few minutes, but the serious business of roaring on the boys in green against Spain intervened, so we arranged to meet up at the same point after the match. Michael had a spare seat in his limousine, so I travelled back to downtown Seoul with Lisa, himself and a few other friends. First port of call was the Westin Chosun Hotel close to the city's main square, which was the Ireland squad's base during their six days in the South Korean capital.

While unwinding over a few drinks in the bar, squad physio Mick Byrne arrived down to invite us upstairs for a meal with the official party. Mick was keen that Michael would meet the players, and Michael was chuffed to accept the invitation. After the meal, Spud commandeered Michael's limo and began to organise the ferrying of the players down to a nearby Irish bar for a few drinks. The bar's landlords were from the counties of Cavan and Cork and were anxious to honour the boys. Flanked by dozens of Ireland fans, the limo made the short journey from the hotel, with Robbie Keane, Damien Duff and Jason McAteer peering out through the sunroof, saluting the boys and girls in green. Michael then arrived down in the limo. ,

After drinking our fill there, we decided to go to a nightclub. But while we were waiting for the limo to return to pick us up, one supporter, who was visibly 'tired and emotional', climbed into the limo through the open sunroof. It quickly became clear that a few words of encouragement were not going to talk him out of the car, so, as unofficial bouncers, Spud and I took charge. It was just as well that we intervened, because Michael, who was a Golden Gloves boxing champion, was about to unleash a nice uppercut. I grabbed his arm and convinced him that diplomacy was still the best option. Eventually, somebody tickled the bloke under the armpits, and he relaxed his grip on the edge of the sunroof and was pulled out.

It was now seven o'clock in the morning and all the clubs were closed. So Michael invited us all back to the Ritz Carlton, where he had one of its plushest suites. We were treated like royalty, with drinks and snacks arriving every few minutes. With the players now fully relaxed, Michael produced his pipe and began to smoke. Michael called for his flute and played a few traditional tunes. Few of us were aware that Michael is also a three-times Irish champion on the flute and has recorded CDs of his music.

Despite the craic, fine food and refreshments, several of the players' minds kept returning to the events of earlier that night in Suwon and their agonising exit from the tournament in a penalty shoot-out. Matt Holland, in particular, was very down on himself. Being such a proud and honourable bloke, Matt misguidedly felt that he had let down his family and the team by missing one of the spot kicks.

Michael decided that they should all have a chat in order to get the disappointment out of their systems. As far as the 'super hoofer' was concerned, nobody was leaving that room until they felt a lot better about themselves. Michael asked the lads to think about the worst thing that had ever happened to them. He told the boys that their setbacks in football were just the same as knocks he had suffered in his business. 'Sure, you're going to feel down in yourself right now,' stated Michael, 'but you've also got to tell yourself that it was great to go so far in the World Cup finals, especially after the furore caused by the Roy Keane situation.'

We all contributed to the conversation and Spud revealed that his darkest hour was when his brother, Michael, was killed in Florida while training as a pilot for Aer Lingus. After Spud spoke, Michael turned again to Matt and told him that losing to Spain wasn't a disaster. 'There are so many people who are proud of you tonight and so many who would like to pat you on the back right now,' Michael told Matt. It was the simplest form of psychology, but it was superb and you could instinctively tell that spirits were being lifted as the chat continued.

Naturally enough, the topic of Roy Keane arose. I was really impressed that not one of the lads ridiculed Roy. Duffer, in particular, was very supportive of Roy and made a point of stating that he regarded him as the best player in the world. 'I just love to play with Roy and I hope he comes back,' he said. What also made these exchanges about Roy all the more intriguing was that they were made in the presence of Mick McCarthy's daughter, Anna. At no point did any of the players criticise or insult the Ireland manager over his role in the Roy Keane affair, yet to a man, they were sorry that Roy had not been with them at the World Cup finals. It was clear to me that they all privately hoped Irish football could move on with Roy back in a team managed by Mick McCarthy.

Duffer was probably the most upbeat player present that night. 'Man, you're a legend and I love to see you dance,' declared Duffer to Michael. 'My mother loves to see you dance.' Michael was having none of it: 'No, no, I'm not the legend – you are. Just think of the cheer you gave to tens of millions of Irish people all over the world during the past few weeks. That's why I don't want to see any of you upset here tonight. You deserve the pats on the back and as far as I'm concerned you are the legends. I'm proud to be Irish, proud of my heritage and proud to sit around this table with you tonight.'

I've no doubt that Michael meant every word of what he said, because he had gone to some trouble to get to Suwon. I know that having your own jet makes life easier, but Michael's busy schedule prevented him from getting to any of the group matches in Japan.

When Michael's debriefing session ended, we started a singsong. Breakfast was then ordered, courtesy of Michael, and what had started out as a night haunted by the demons of Suwon ended with Irish eyes smiling once more. It was midday before we finally left Michael's suite and there's no doubt that the players all felt much more positive. They may have been goosed with tiredness, but mentally they were now dealing positively with their World Cup experience rather than dwelling on the way the team exited.

We have all met people in life who are 'great' on the first acquaintance but the next time round have changed. Not Michael. When he turned around to see who was behind him in the stadium in Suwon, it was if we had only been separated for a week. He was delighted to see me and I was overjoyed with his welcome. I felt that he wanted to acknowledge that I had taken care of him all those years ago. In fact, he almost embarrassed me!

People may say that Michael is full of himself – and remember, this is a part of his business – but I have only positive things to say about his manner. As far as I am concerned, he's down to earth, loves his pint and is a class man. His love of Ireland and its culture is not a marketing gimmick – it's heartfelt and stems from his upbringing in the States. He promotes this country every opportunity he gets.

Since that night in Suwon, Michael and I have kept in touch. I have visited him at his Irish country retreat at Castlehyde, outside Fermoy in County Cork. I also went to the party to celebrate his engagement to Lisa in another of his homes in Nice. 'Any chance of getting a few kegs of Guinness down to Nice from Dublin?' enquired Michael about a month before the big night. I was chuffed that Michael had called upon my expertise to ensure that the pints of Guinness were up to the required standard on the Côte d'Azur.

This was a task that needed the combined brainpower of Spud and myself, so we sat down one evening and worked out a strategy on how to get four barrels of creamy stout and a cooler from St James' Gate to the shores of the Mediterranean. With the help of Gibneys pub in Malahide, Spud and myself produced a plan of action for 'Operation Arthur'. Spud found a courier capable of delivering the kegs and the cooler to Michael's house at 11 o'clock on the morning of the party. I had arrived in Nice a few days earlier with Melanie.

At lunchtime on the day of the party, I went to Michael's pad to set up the Guinness bar. With Bono's house perched just a short distance below and Elton John's gaff a little bit further up the road,

I really felt that I was in the playground of the rich and famous. Michael's house is situated on a hill, and has an incredible view of the city out into the bay. The grounds of Michael's house are breathtaking, with a swimming pool cut into the side of the hill. It's a truly fabulous house; you even need to take an elevator to get up to the front door!

When I got to the house, we took a few minutes to enjoy a coffee and sandwich. 'We'll set up the bar outside,' said Michael.

'Grand, where's the bar?' I asked, to be told that there was none.

'We'll make one up,' Michael told me. So, off I toddled to source the materials needed to construct a bar.

First port of call was his gym, where I gathered up as many of the steel bars that could be taken from the various pieces of equipment. I managed to drag out a few planks of wood from a pile of builder's leftovers at the side of the house. We were getting there. Michael's housekeepers supplied a couple of white sheets, and we managed to build the bar. Now I had to set up the keg, cooler and tap. I had never rigged up a cooler like this before, so I got on the phone to Spud – a man of many tricks – back in Dublin, who directed me on how to assemble it. I then let it sit for a few hours before I pulled the first pint, as per Spud's advice.

While we were waiting for the Guinness to settle, we took a dip in the pool, me sweating less from the sun overhead and more in the hope that all was going to work out to plan. But, thank God, the first pint flowed like a dream. Michael savoured it as he lounged in his pool overlooking the Mediterranean. His joy was matched only by my relief. That wasn't the last pint I served that day. My services were called upon later in the celebrations, when it became clear that the catering firm's five-star expertise in delivering the finest foods and wines did not extend to pulling pints of plain. As any Guinness drinker will tell you, the famous brew from Dublin can be made almost undrinkable if the bartender fails to let it pour at the right speed and angle from the tap.

I sensed something was slightly amiss when I noticed Michael scratching his head as he sipped another pint. So there was nothing for it but for me to take off my jacket and tear into the task myself – but I always made sure that I had a pint beside me as well!

Paul Harrington, the former Ireland Eurovision winner, supplied the music at the party. It was a lovely occasion that was held mainly for the Flatley and Murphy families, close friends and the staff from Castlehyde. While the press was asked along, it wasn't a parade of international celebrities.

Lisa and Michael made a lovely couple and got on so well together, so I was very surprised when they split earlier this year. Lisa never forgot about her roots in Dublin, and treated people as equals no matter what walk of life they hailed from. Michael is the same – his caretaker at Castlehyde, Pat Bartley, would regularly be asked to sit down for dinner with him.

It's a pity that Lisa and himself won't be settling down to married life in Castlehyde. The County Cork mansion may be short of a woman of the house right now, but its renovation remains a lasting tribute to Michael's commitment to Ireland. Four years ago, Michael bought the 30,000 square-foot house for €4 million. I was given the guided tour just as the architects, craftsmen and builders entered the crumbling ruin, so I know what he's managed to achieve.

He invested €50m on the refurbishment. In doing so, people will soon realise how much he has contributed to the heritage of this nation. It made my blood boil to hear a few months back that some people were giving him a hard time over the matter of a small pond in the front garden. Take it from me, Castlehyde was a dive when I first saw it. It would probably have required demolition in a few years' time but for Michael's intervention. It's no surprise that the locals are right behind him. He's put Fermoy on the map and also gives generously to events and groups in the area.

I was once given a special tour of the White House in Washington, but it would hardly live with Castlehyde. That's a tribute to Michael's vision, plus the combined talents of architect Peter Inston and project manager David Higgins. I'm looking forward to spending some time down there over the coming years, walking the estate, with Michael carrying the blackthorn stick I gave him last year. Big Jack is lined up for a spot of fishing on the Blackwater River, which runs by the house.

14

BOSTON'S CELT COLLINS

THEY say that Boston is the 33rd county of Ireland. Like those living in the 32 counties, the citizens of Boston live, eat and breathe sport. Be it supporting the Boston Celts in basketball, the New England Patriots in American football, the Boston Bruins in ice hockey, the Boston Red Socks in baseball or the New England Revolution soccer team, Bostonians have a passion for sport that covers all classes, colours and creeds.

During the 1960s, the Celts ruled the NBA, while Larry Bird and the team of the 1970s and early 1980s gave the city a feeling of nationwide supremacy. The Patriots have won their share of Super Bowls and are the reigning champions, and is there a more famous baseball arena on the planet than the quaint Fenway Park?

The immigrant Irish have always supported Boston's sports stars, but when one of their own emerged in the mid and late-1980s as a contender in the tough battleground of the boxing business, it gave them that extra sense of pride. Steve Collins was that man and Bostonians, both Irish and non-Irish alike, hailed the man from Annamoe Terrace in Dublin's Cabra as their own. In return, Collins spoke proudly of the fact that Boston gave him his chance of glory in the world of professional boxing.

In late 1986 and early 1987, the word amongst the Boston Irish was that Steve could go places. He was training with the Petronelli brothers, who were regarded as two of the best trainers in the business. Back in the 1970s and 1980s, the Petronellis had trained the great Marvin Hagler, who held the world middleweight title for seven years. That was one hell of a reputation to hang your hat on.

'Marvellous' Marvin was popular with the Irish, and I actually met him one day through unusual circumstances. One Saturday morning, when I was working for Cunningham Electrical, I was down in the boss Tom Mitchell's house in Hannover in Boston, a few doors up from where Hagler lived. I was in the garage when I noticed a few pigeons up in the loft. Shortly afterwards, this guy walked up the driveway and asked whether I had seen any of his pigeons. I did a double take before I confirmed to myself that it was Hagler. We had a short chat before he retrieved his pigeons.

Steve was determined to succeed. Taken under the wing of boxing patron Marty Ward, another northside Dublin exile from the North Circular Road, Steve was blossoming as he combined his part-time jobs with the serious business of building up a credible boxing career. Steve was working for a good friend of mine, Pete Nash, down in his bar in Dorchester. Steve was holding the fort one afternoon, when he received a phone call from one of the Petronellis asking him to get down to the gym as soon as possible. There was no other staff on duty, so Steve asked one of the trusted regulars to take over, telling him that he would be back in a while!

When we opened up the Blackthorn in 1990, Steve was training in a gym on L Street. Part of his regime was a daily run, after which he would call into the pub for a pint of water. We enjoyed a chat and he often told me that his ambition was to scrape about $100,000 together to build a nice house in Dublin for his family. Then he would go back to his trade as an electrician.

I was at nearly all of his early professional fights in the US. Steve suffered his first professional defeat against his great rival Mike McCallum in the Boston Gardens in February 1990. In November of that year, Steve fought Eddie Hall in Boston and defeated him in 10 rounds. A TV deal to cover the fight fell through, so I bought the rights from Steve and arranged the videotaping of the bout. We agreed that the video would be shown in the Blackthorn after the fight, so I organised for a limo decked out in the Irish colours to bring the Collins entourage back to the bar.

I turned cameraman for the night. I was thrilled with the shots I got with my camcorder, as Steve had told the promoters to give me as much access as possible. In fact, I almost sustained a few blows as I stretched too close to the ropes.

During the bill, there was an unexpected and thrilling bonus for me, when I was introduced to the great Jake La Motta, who was in the crowd. Back in the late 1940s and early 1950s, La Motta was a legend as a fighter, but he enjoyed an even bigger degree of celebrity after the release of Martin Scorsese's 1980 film *Raging Bull*, which was based on his life. With Robert de Niro in the leading role as La Motta, *Raging Bull* is still regarded as the best sport's film ever made. So, when Jake joined us down in the Blackthorn later that night, I reckon I floated in the front door.

Not surprisingly, there were queues right down West Broadway that night. We did our best to cram in as many people as possible, while ensuring we kept the fire authorities happy. I was talking to Jake, when I received word that Steve wanted to see me as quickly as possible. 'I haven't got a red cent on me and all my family are here,' said Steve. I assured him that the drinks' bill was on the house, but he insisted that he still required a few dollars. Steve asked for $400, which I readily gave him. His presence had guaranteed that the Blackthorn was stuffed to the gills.

After establishing himself in Boston and the US, Steve returned to Dublin. When he appeared on *The Late Late Show*, people said he came across as cocky and arrogant. But that was simply the injection of American self-confidence that goes with the territory of professional boxing. You cannot go into the ring against a strong opponent with the wishy-washy feeling that you 'might' win the fight. In the professional game, you always believe that you 'will' win. To watch Steve Collins training and preparing for his big fight nights was a lesson to us all on how to adopt the right attitude. Nobody could ever convince him that he was not going to succeed.

What made Steve so popular with the Irish in Boston – apart from the obvious fact that he was born in Dublin and was proud of his roots – was the realisation that Steve and his now ex-wife, Gemma, had battled against adversity from the moment they set foot on American soil in 1986. Like many of the fans who were packing out his shows in Boston and, increasingly beyond Massachusetts in Atlantic City and Las Vegas, Steve and Gemma had held down three and four jobs in order to survive. Steve didn't get anything for nothing, and all that he achieved he got the hard way. Irish pub owners recognised that inner determination and talent, and were only too happy to rally around with financial backing with advertisements in his fight programmes.

Following his move to the Barry Hearn management team in London in the early 1990s, Steve fell out with the Petronellis. Court writs began to fly, and at one stage he was told that he might not be able to fight again in the US, where the big money is. Thankfully he did return to the US, after his success in Europe. That row rumbled on for a while, and one night about four years later in the Baggot Inn in Dublin a fella came over and tried to hand Steve a brown paper envelope. Steve put out his hand, but intentionally missed it, knowing that the envelope probably contained a court order.

Unfortunately, Steve upset a lot of his fans in Boston when his December 1994 fight with Lonny Beasley in the Boston Gardens was called off just two days before the scheduled bout. Many felt that the explanation that he was ill fell short, and that annoyed quite a few punters who had been loyal to him for the best part of a decade. I later learned that he had indeed picked up the dreaded streptococcal virus, which leaves you feeling as if you've been hit with the worst 'flu of your life, so he had no option but to call off the fight.

That didn't stop a member of the Collins' clan appearing on the bill that night and writing himself into Boston's boxing lore. Steve's younger brother, Paschal, was beginning to make a name for himself as a boxer. He was included on the bill as the 'swing' bout, which means that the promoter will stick the fight in on the card when and where is possible. As the night progressed, the promoter Al Valenti informed Paschal's camp that there was no time for his fight. That didn't go down too well, as a large number of his family and friends had travelled over from Dublin for the event.

Thanks to the intervention of a few people, including respected *Irish Star* boxing writer Gerry Callan, Valenti relented and Paschal's fight was marked down as the last on the card. Paschal defeated his opponent after just 24 seconds – a record for the Boston Gardens. It was the last-ever fight at the famous venue, before it was torn down by the demolition men to make way for the Boston Forum.

I missed Steve's famous first showdown with Chris Eubank in Millstreet, County Cork, in March 1995, as I needed to attend a number of business matters back in Boston. I arranged for the show to be beamed into the Blackthorn, where the then Minister for Communications Michael Lowry and several senior RTÉ executives were amongst the customers. We shouted ourselves hoarse that night, as Steve ended Eubank's unbeaten record, and added the WBO super middleweight crown to the WBO middleweight title he had secured by beating Britain's Chris Pyatt the previous year.

After finding myself 3,000 miles from the action that night, there was no way I was going to miss the rematch in Páirc Uí Chaoimh the following September. Frank and John Smith from the Submarine bar in Dublin ordered two helicopters to ferry down the gang from Dublin. Frank Smith, Eddie Furey, Paddy Reilly and two Heineken sales reps joined me in one chopper, while John Smith and members of his family travelled in the other. We arrived in style at the Silver Springs Hotel in Cork city.

Steve was at the height of his powers in the ring. Eubank had built his career on bluffing his way past opponents, but Steve completely out-psyched him with his pre-fight talk. He had Eubank tied up in knots before a punch had been thrown, and his employment of mind guru Tony Quinn in the corner was a masterstroke. Eubank didn't know whether to cry with frustration, as he lost again, or laugh with joy as his torment came to an end. The official records show that the judges' verdict was a split decision, but everybody gathered in the famous stadium had long since given the Dubliner the fight. The points count showed that they were right. That night, Jury's Hotel in Cork heaved like it has never done before or since, as the Collins' victory party swang into action.

On the way back the following afternoon, Ciaran Haughey found out that he would be unable to land the helicopter back in Dublin for a few hours, as an electrical storm had done damage to the control tower at the airport. When the pilot enquired as to our next move, Frank Smith made the decision: 'Drop us in Tyrrellspass where we'll have a pint with Gillespie's old fella.' So up over Munster and the south midlands we went, crossing Ballyporeen, Tullamore and Kilbeggan, before finally spotting Tyrrellspass castle in the distance. 'Where will we land the chopper?' asked Ciaran.

I felt that the famous village green was too near the main road, so I suggested the GAA pitch on the Mullingar Road. However, after doing a circle of the town in honour of the people below and me, the returning 'prodigal son', the former Taoiseach's son opted for the small football pitch behind the school. I had phoned my old friend Martin O'Brien in advance, and he picked up the Colonel in his limo and then collected us from the school. We headed up to Sheridan's pub, as it was called at the time, and sank a few pints of porter. Paddy and Eddie gave us a singsong, and the Colonel even sang us his favourite song, 'Paddy Caherly', about a local man who once ran for election.

My father had a great time. You've heard of brassed-off bus drivers rounding up stragglers from pubs on trips back home from football matches, well poor old Ciaran was forced to intervene, warning us that he needed to get the helicopter back to Dublin before dark. When we finally took off, I could see my father's face as he gazed up in amazement. My only regret was that my mother had not been there to see us, but I'm sure she was looking down from above and minding us.

A few days after the successful retention of his title, Steve joined a gang of us – who included Olympic boxing gold medallist Michael Carruth, Patsy Watchorn of Dublin City Ramblers, Seán Keane of the Chieftains, Brendan Grace and Jack Charlton – for a celebration in Frank Smith's house. Frank's brother John had all of Steve's gear in the car, so I dressed up in Steve's top and cloak and then had the gloves tied up. Big Jack challenged me to 'three rounds' on the floor of Frank's sitting-room. I decided to give my 'opponent' a small tip, but whatever way I connected with him I left him sitting on the seat of his pants!

The Collins' road show rolled on, and he successfully defended his crown against Cornelius Carr in Dublin in November of that year, then Neville Brown in Millstreet in early 1996, before twice beating the dangerous Nigel Benn in Manchester in 1996. My next excursion to watch Steve was in February 1997, when he took care of Frenchman Frederic Sellier in nine rounds at London's Docklands Arena, in what would prove to be his second-last fight. His farewell bout was a win over Craig Cummings in Glasgow the following July.

Jason McAteer and Phil Babb linked up with me in Jury's hotel in Kensington for the London fight, along with their Liverpool team-mate Stan Collymore. The Liverpool team was flying at the time and was battling with Manchester United for the Premiership title. The two lads were less than pleased with Stan, who arrived very late at Jury's, and they gave him a right earful. Stan muttered some excuse about bumping into an old friend. So, throwing the ticket at Stan, we all headed off for east London by taxi, anxious to get there in time to see Prince Naseem Hamed's fight, who was on the early section of the bill.

The Prince won his fight, and with Steve still on a roll, there was a huge party back in Jury's. There may have been hundreds of Irish people there that night, but the staff in the hotel were almost as good as my own back in the Blackthorn. Steve introduced me to a number of his other friends, and he even told them about the night that he borrowed the $400 off me. 'I thought you had forgotten all about it, and I never liked to ask you about it,' I said. 'But now that you brought it up, how are you fixed?' Needless to say I got the deaf ear, but I was only joking.

15

Larry Drops in for a Pint

MENTION the Baggot Inn in Dublin to any music fan in Ireland, and they'll quickly let you know that it was regarded as one of the cradles of the nation's rock and pop industry. Drop the name Larry Mullen into a conversation with anybody with the merest interest in rock and roll, and they will instantly reply that the man concerned is the drummer with U2. For me, I have been lucky enough to have co-owned the Baggot – as it's known to all – while I can count upon Larry as a friend. Larry may be a multi-millionaire rockstar, but he remains a quiet, unassuming man.

My own involvement with the Baggot was half planned, half hit and miss. Over the years, Jack Charlton and I had many casual conversations about opening a pub together in Dublin. In 1994, we decided to sit down and talk about it seriously. By that time, the Blackthorn was flying, thanks to the hard work of the staff, the long hours put in by Chris and myself and the solid support of our customers. We had made enough money to invest in another pub. Frank Smith of the famous Submarine bar in Dublin said he'd look around for a pub for us in Dublin.

Through the grapevine, Frank's brother, John, heard that Jimmy McGettigan might be interested in selling the Baggot Inn. The boys didn't want to contact Jimmy, because it was well known that they were friends with Jack. They were afraid that Jimmy might put the price up a little higher if he suspected Jack was involved. I made the arrangements to meet Jimmy. Afterwards, when the deal was done, Jimmy said that if he had known who was involved he 'might have made an extra few bob!' But being the lovely man he is, he admitted that he didn't care. 'I'm happy enough and I wish you the best of luck,' he told me, and he was true to his word. As we were doing work in the Baggot ahead of the opening, Jimmy came in one day, shook all our hands and sent us up a barrel of Guinness and a barrel of Smithwicks for a drink.

We were all excited at the prospect of taking over one of Dublin's best-known pubs. Over the years, all of Ireland's greatest musicians and bands had played in the Baggot: from U2 to the Fureys and Davy Arthur and from the Dubliners to Thin Lizzy. Even though the famous back bar was small and cramped, it more than made up for it with its unique atmosphere and reputation as one of the best live venues in Europe.

After paying about £1.2 million (approximately €1.5 million) for the pub, it was important that we made a big success of the venture. While Dublin pubs regularly sell for three and four times that figure now, it was a large price to pay for the Baggot. Unfortunately, the news that Jimmy McGettigan was selling his pub was interpreted by some people as the death knell for live music in the Baggot. Soon newspaper articles appeared suggesting that this was the case. Naturally there was a big outcry about Jack Charlton getting involved in the Baggot Inn and ending the music era in it. I was shocked, because one of our reasons for purchasing the pub was to encourage live music – a policy that was central to the Blackthorn's success and something that was close to my heart.

Flying in from Boston one morning, I was greeted with the headlines that this was 'the last night of music in the Baggot Inn'. It was crucial that we got the word out that we were going to continue with live music. We booked Dickie Rock for the opening night of the 'New Baggot' and the place was humming. One of the Aer Lingus pilots who had flown me home a few days earlier, and whom I had chatted to in the cockpit, turned up with a bunch of his mates, en route to a party elsewhere. But Dickie's show was so good, they cancelled their later engagement and told the rest of the partygoers to get down to the Baggot.

Within weeks, the Fureys and several other big names had appeared at the Baggot. We had firmly scotched the notion that live music had been banished from the pub. During those first few months, I would receive the occasional late-night phone call from Larry Mullen after a hard day's work in Windmill Lane studios: 'Frankie, I'm just coming out of the studio – is there any chance of a beer, or is it too late?' 'Larry, it's never too late for you to have a beer in the Baggot,' was my standard reply.

Myself and Jack's son, John, were managing the pub. I was enjoying life in the city, even if I was back and forth across the Atlantic to do my bit in the Blackthorn. One day, Jack, Paddy Reilly, myself and Larry Mullen were having a beer at the bar, talking about music and the rich history of the Baggot. Larry told us that after he played in the Baggot as a teenager with U2, he would always have to get out of the place fairly fast because if he didn't catch the last bus home he'd have got into trouble with his father.

Paddy asked him: 'How much were yous getting at that time, Larry?'

'Twenty quid a night. We often backed you up, Paddy'. replied Larry.

Paddy told him that he got around £30 a night. Larry then said to him: 'You're not playing for £30 now, Paddy'.

'Well,' said Paddy, as he put his glass down on the counter, 'yous aren't playing for £20 either!'

The Baggot soon became firmly established as a pub where sports people and sports lovers could congregate for a drink. And 1995 proved to be a great year on the Gaelic football front, with Dublin winning the Sam Maguire and my own beloved Westmeath triumphing in the All Ireland minor final on the same day. A few weeks before the finals, Dubs legend Jimmy Keaveney called in for a few pints of stout. 'Whatever you do, put a few bob on that

Westmeath team to win the minor,' said Jimmy. 'It's a grand little team. I've watched them make great progress at Croker this year.'

I was all set for Croke Park on that third Sunday in September to see the Westmeath minors lift the county's first All Ireland title at either minor or senior level. Mick Byrne had got me a ticket. But all my plans were scratched when I landed up in bed with a dreadful dose of the 'flu. I just about managed to watch the second half of the senior match on the Baggot's television.

On the following Wednesday night in Croke Park, the victorious senior Dublin team played the traditional GOAL challenge charity match against the Rest of Ireland Selection. One of the Baggot barmen, Padraig Keane, a son of the Chieftains' Seán Keane, and I went to see the game. The match was abandoned about 15 minutes from the end, when hundreds of kids ran onto the pitch to mob Jason Sherlock, who was the pin-up boy of the Dubs' team at the time.

Afterwards, we bumped into Dublin star Keith Barr, who was a good friend of ours in the Baggot. Keith managed to get myself and Padraig into the dressing-room to meet all the players. I asked Keith and the lads whether they were going for a pint up to Hanlon's – a famous Dublin GAA pub at Hanlon's corner – because that was the normal haunt after matches. 'No, there's nothing arranged,' said Keith. 'Maybe we'll go back to the Baggot.' So the bould Keith got everybody arranged and we all went back to the Baggot. I made a quick phone call to get a band to play that night.

It turned out to be one of those amazing nights. Meath legend and television critic Colm O'Rourke was there, as was Tyrone's Peter Canavan and many other stars from all over Ireland. Everybody took their turn to sing up on the stage, including, at one point, the whole Dublin team. Steve Collins came over and sang a few songs. I think that Charlie Redmond was the last one I threw out at five o'clock in the morning.

***

Pat Kenny used the Baggot as one of the venues for Big Jack's 'This Is Your Life' on *The Late Late Show* in 1996. Of course, when they were planning the show, Pat's producers had not reckoned on the likes of Aldo and Larry Mullen! The boys were supposed to come out to the RTÉ studio to meet us in the audience before the start of the show, but when we looked at the television monitor they were still in the Baggot, from where part of the show was being broadcast. Thankfully, a speedy taxi and a timely advert break allowed the boys to get out to Montrose for the second part of the show. Many of Jack's best friends and a few of his heroes were flown in by RTÉ, and he really enjoyed that night.

Jack's biggest football hero, the great John Charles, came over. The Welshman, who died earlier this year, played as centre half and striker for Wales, Leeds United and Juventus and was at Elland Road for a short time when Jack began his career at the club.

Larry Mullen was particularly thrilled to be called upon to say a few words, as he has travelled the world over supporting the Irish team. Larry's the real football fan in U2, even though their Cork-born soundman Joe O'Herlihy – a committed Cork City and Manchester United supporter – would claim he knows more than the drummer about the game!

My own relationship with Larry dates back to the time we were on the team bus going to a game in Lansdowne Road in 1993. The traditional singsong was in full flow, with 'The Fields of Athenry' and 'Sean South from Garryowen' blasting out. John Charlton brought me up to meet Larry, and we got on brilliantly. People might question why the drummer from one of the biggest bands in the world was on the Ireland team bus. But that just showed how Big Jack was able to ease the tension ahead of game by creating a relaxed environment. Larry was very friendly with Andy Townsend, Kevin Moran and many of the older players, but he got on great with everybody. Naturally, the players never had a problem securing a ticket for a U2 concert or for the after-show drinks.

When he's in Boston, Larry always drops into the Blackthorn for a pint, and he's been the perfect host to me and my kids at several U2 concerts. During the Elevation Tour in 2001, myself and my son, Trevor, travelled over to Anaheim in California where U2 played three concerts in the famous Mighty Duck's Stadium. Joe O'Herlihy walked out to meet us and gave us a packet of tickets for the week. Larry was after taking care of the whole thing with backstage passes to all the concerts, where we got the opportunity to rub shoulders with all the celebrities.

Myself and Trevor took in the three concerts. We partied with Cameron Diaz, Robbie Williams, Meg Ryan, Samantha Mumba and even ended up dancing with Salman Rushdie. I would have been in danger if someone had taken a pot shot at Salman! I had met Robbie Williams before, with Jason McAteer and Phil Babb at Paul McGrath's testimonial in Dublin. I thought he was a bit mad at the time, but I approached him anyway that night in Anaheim. I told him that I had met him with Jason and Phil eight years earlier. He immediately put his arm around me and walked me straight to the bar for a drink. He could not have been nicer to Trevor and myself. He actually went to the trouble of bringing us backstage half an hour before the show and talked to us for about ten minutes before posing for photographs.

My daughter, Donna, and myself made the short trip to New York to catch U2 at Madison Square Gardens. And that also turned out to be a night to remember. After the gig, Donna ended up dancing with Tiger Woods. I shook hands with him, slipped a card into his hand and said: 'Tiger, if you're ever in Boston come into the Blackthorn bar.' Afterwards back in the bar, the story did the rounds that Tiger's career went into a nosedive due to his encounter with me, because in the following weeks he finished a few tournaments down the field.

In all, I probably went to about ten Elevation Tour gigs around the States. I was at one in Miami, one in New York, three in

Boston and one in Providence, Rhode Island. Myself and Brendan Grace went to the show at the Fleet Centre in Boston in June 2001. Paddy Reilly was also due to go to the gig, but wasn't feeling too good that night and had to go to bed. My young fella's friend, who was mad into U2, got the spare ticket. Little did he know that after the show that he was going to meet the band!

Joe invited us all back to the Four Seasons Hotel, even though Brendan was a bit reluctant, feeling that he might be crowding the band. When we got out of the elevator, the first one to meet us was U2 manager, Paul McGuinness. 'Oh my God, Brendan, how are you?' said Paul with a broad smile, as he came over and put his arms around him. Paul then brought us into the room where the lads were. He told us there was a free bar, and we needed no second invitation. When Brendan needed a cigarette, we went out into the corridor. Larry came out after us: 'What are yez doing out here?' 'We're smoking, for f***'s sake,' replied Brendan. Larry put his arms around Brendan and thanked him for coming up. Then the Edge came over, followed by Bono. They each gave Brendan a big hug, and Brendan was really chuffed that the lads knew so much about him.

We had a great night, and a few days later Larry came down to the Boston Baggot to watch Ireland play Estonia in a World Cup qualifier in Tallinn. As we often do for big games, Chris and myself had ordered in live satellite coverage for the customers in the Blackthorn. But given the special guest who was joining us in the Baggot, I asked the cable network Setanta to supply the game to our other pub.

We enjoyed a couple of pints, and Ireland won 2–0. Afterwards the *Boston Herald* wrote a feature which mentioned the event: 'While Larry Mullen was watching his favourite Irish team play in the World Cup against Estonia, Bono was at Harvard giving a speech to the students.'

Larry is the member of U2 who I'm best acquainted with, but I know that the rest of the lads – Bono, the Edge and Adam Clayton – are all top men. When you're speaking to Bono, he gives you his undivided attention. My young fella, Trevor, plays lead guitar in his own band called Roxie. He had a great chat with the Edge, and was thrilled with the advice that came his way.

After U2's final concert in Boston, myself, Spud, his brother Barney and a few friends were all in the Baggot having a drink. We had all been at the Fleet Centre and were reflecting on the band's impact on the city once again. Then we got a phone call from Larry to say he was on his way in a cab, after ditching his own security. I was slightly nervous that Larry's visit might be ruined by autograph hunters. However, Larry displayed all his down-to-earth qualities and shook as many hands as were extended his way. The barmen and the punters were all given some of his time. When he was leaving the bar that night, they all stood up and gave him a round of applause.

Larry and myself still stay in contact, and there's nothing more I like than having a pint with him in Gibneys of Malahide. He's on first-name terms with all the old-timers in Gibneys. Even though Larry loves New York, I get the distinct feeling that he still is at his most comfortable back in his hometown of Dublin.

We sold the Baggot in Dublin in 1998 and made a few bob for ourselves. It's since been levelled by the new owners. I don't think we'll ever experience a repeat of those great nights of music in the Baggot Inn. They were something special.

16

PÁIDÍ DELIVERS THE HOLY GRAIL

I have benefited from my love of soccer with friendships with Jack Charlton, Mick Byrne, Denis Irwin, Kevin Moran, John Aldridge and Steve Staunton, but I have been equally rewarded for my passion for Gaelic games and, in particular, Gaelic football. Be it in Tyrrellspass, London or Boston, I've never been too far away from the action as a player, official or fan.

For as long as I can remember, Gaelic football has been a central part of life for me, my brothers and my friends. When we were young, we would gather in our dozens on the village green to kick a ball about. As a 13-year-old full back, I was on the combined Tyrrellspass-Rochfortbridge team that won the under-14 county championship, beating Castletown Finea by four points to three. However, Castletown claimed that we fielded a couple of over-age players and a special minor board meeting in Mullingar awarded the cup to the opposition.

The cup sat proudly in Maher's window in the village for a few weeks, and the junior team – who were beaten in their county final that same day by St Malachy's – were full of praise for us. Three years later, my brother Eugene was on the team that won the club's first-ever adult county championship.

In 1974, I got my footballing break: one Sunday afternoon, I was in the squad for the Round Towers team in London, when one of the forwards was injured. I came on for him with about 15 minutes to go and scored two goals to help the side to victory. I was the first to congratulate our midfield star, the great Tommy Greene who played for Offaly against Down in the 1961 All-Ireland senior final and whose hard work set up both scoring chances. However, as a raw 17-year-old, I got the attention and the minor selectors added me to the London squad. I got a free trip home to Ireland and a chance to play Cavan in Croke Park in the All Ireland minor football quarter-final. The Ulster champions were too strong for us on the day, and beat us by six points. Although I ended up on the losing side, that was one of the happiest days of my life. Many a great player has never ventured onto the hallowed Croke Park turf.

As kids, Mick Carley was our footballing hero. He had joined the Tyrrellspass club from the Downs, who were traditionally one of the big powers in senior football in Westmeath. Mick had played for Leinster in the Railway Cup, which was no mean feat for a man from one of the weaker footballing counties. Mick's presence in the Tyrrellspass team gave the entire village a lift. Luckily, I was involved in the same intermediate squad as Mick when we reached the 1975 county final. St Malachy's edged us out, 1–7 to 0–9.

From 1978 onwards, my playing days with Tyrrellspass were constantly interrupted by frequent excursions to Boston. I suppose losing players to emigration was a curse that afflicted every club in Ireland during the 1980s. A few smaller clubs even had to fold because of it. But Tyrrellspass weathered that storm and progressed from being a junior outfit to enjoying lengthy spells in both the senior and intermediate ranks. After 15 years of blood, sweat and tears from many people in the area, the club's splendid new grounds, Páirc Naomh Stiofáin, were officially opened in May 1991, by the then GAA president, Peter Quinn. Walking around the pitch and clubrooms today, I still feel proud to have played with the club.

The new grounds seem to have spurred the club on to even greater success, and in 1999 Tyrrellspass won the Westmeath senior football championship for the first time. Many teams had departed the village for Cusack Park in Mullingar over the years with the order to bring the Flanagan Cup back 'over the Chapel Hill'. Captain John O'Brien fulfilled that dream, with a 2–6 to 1–7 victory over the champions, Athlone. That win put Tyrrellspass on the Gaelic football map throughout Ireland. As John O'Brien said in his victory speech after lifting the cup aloft, 'We'll no longer be called the lilywhites of Westmeath football'. This long-awaited win was followed five years later with the breakthrough at senior county level.

***

After playing Gaelic football in Tyrrellspass and then later in London, it was only natural that I should hook up with a club in Boston when I moved there. In fact, one of the attractions about life in the States was the Gaelic football scene. For many years, dating from when I first worked in Boston in 1978, I played with the St Pat's senior team, which was based mainly in the Brighton area and trained in St John's College.

There were great fellas involved in football in Boston, and they really helped me to settle in the States. Men like Mike Connor, Pat Blythe and Chris Sullivan looked after me and made sure that I had a day's pay in my pocket. However, when I was working for Mike Connor, I fell off a ladder and hurt my back, which meant I couldn't train for a couple of weeks. I was demoted to the St Pat's junior team, where I was appointed captain. But the injury persisted and I was unable to play for another two weeks, so the selectors removed the captaincy from me.

I probably didn't see eye to eye with them too much after that. In 1987, St Pat's won the junior championship in Boston, and I was still slightly bitter because, as captain, I should have been the one accepting the cup on behalf of the team. Winning the junior title in Boston allowed us to compete in the All American championships, which were being held in Pittsburgh that year.

However, that only led to more tension between me and the club's officers. At the game, I was left standing on the sideline, while a crowd of lads, who had been at a wedding in Chicago the previous day and who had then driven the whole way from Chicago to Pittsburgh, got picked for the team. With about 15 minutes to go, St Pat's was down by five or six points. They asked me to go on, but I was so annoyed that I refused. We lost the match.

I didn't even go back to Boston with the team, and ended up flying home with Father Tom's hurling team. St Pat's hurlers beat Limerick of Chicago in their final. The famous All Ireland final referee, Seamus Aldridge of Kildare, was the man in charge for their match. I knew Seamus well because I used to sell him oil a few years previously when I worked for Mallen Oil. During my visits to Seamus' house, I often stopped for a cup of tea. So on the day of the final, I went over and shook hands with him. Seamus immediately asked me to 'do the line'.

The Limerick linesman on the far side was giving everything to the Chicago team, no matter what went out, so I made sure things were evened up on my side of the pitch. At one stage of the match, we were down a few points, even though the great Dick O'Hara of Thomastown in Kilkenny was playing with us, as were future Offaly All Ireland senior medal winners, Daithí Regan and Michael Duignan. It was time that Frankie took charge. When a clear-cut Limerick line ball went out on my side, I flagged it for our lads. Despite the Limerick howls of protest, Daithí lobbed the sideline cut into the goalmouth and the sliotar ended up in the back of the net.

Father Tom's side went on to win the match thanks to this crucial goal. At the end of the match, instead of carrying one of their team-mates shoulder high around the pitch, they carted me around! By this stage, Seamus Aldridge had made a hasty exit, because he hadn't known that I was a supporter of Father Tom's team!

On my arrival home from Pittsburgh, I was determined that I'd get a team together to beat St Pat's. One night in 1998, I was sitting in my house one night with Brendan Lenehan, when I announced to him that we were going to start our own team. We began to scribble down names of lads who could carry a bag or who couldn't carry a bag, never mind a jersey. 'I think at this stage we should leave it 'til next year,' said Brendan. 'It's fresh in my head now, and I'm afraid that if it goes to next year it'll never be done,' I argued. 'We're going to get a team, we're going to get X amount of players, we're going to register them and we're going to have our own team,' I added. We decided on the name Wolfe Tones for the club and chose the blue and white colours of Tyrrellspass for the jerseys.

What made me twice as determined to start up our own club was the cock-up that occurred after the finals in Pittsburgh, when the players were unable to get a meal during the evening celebrations. I refused to pay for my ticket for the after-match event. But when we went to register Wolfe Tones, the powers that be told us that in order to do so, we would have to pay the money for a meal we never got! I had to bite the bullet and pay the couple of hundred bucks for the tickets just to register the team. We started off in the junior ranks and, lo and behold, who were we drawn against in the first round of the Boston junior championship, but St Pat's!

We had a fella on our team by the name of Peter Farrell, who had played senior football for the Meath club Seneschalstown. A few days before the game against St Pat's, Peter's aunt died. When I heard he was flying home for the funeral, I went out to the airport and gave him a couple of hundred dollars and said: 'Whatever you do, Peter, make sure you're back for the game on Sunday.' We got back Peter for the game, and he played a stormer. We beat St Pat's by nine points. What's more, I won a few bob on bets and got my money back for the famous tickets.

Football is taken very seriously by the Irish in the US. I almost ended up being barred from one part of Boston, because of a row at a challenge match against Springfield. One of their backs had nailed me a couple of times, but I was very firm and was able to take the tackles. We ended up tussling on the ground and he didn't go for the ball at all. He got me by the hair but I jumped up very quickly. Whatever way I hit him, I did a lot of damage to his jaw. He was carried off, and afterwards I was warned never to go to Springfield again. It reached the stage where there was a possible lawsuit against me, but the local GAA hierarchy sorted it out.

Funnily enough, we were drawn against Springfield in the first round of the junior championship the following year. The phone calls started with warnings to 'tell Gillespie that he'd better not go near Springfield'. But that was a red flag to a bull, and when I arrived in Springfield no one said anything. My 'friend' was still around, but nothing happened on the pitch, and afterwards we even enjoyed a few drinks down in their local bar, the John Boyle O'Reilly.

The Wolfe Tones were beaten in two junior semifinals. We were then re-graded to intermediate level. We were beaten in an intermediate final. We had a very dedicated crew of lads with us that year, with Paul Meade, a neighbour of Colm O'Rourke's from County Meath, the captain.

By 1998, I was no longer centrally involved with the Wolfe Tones. One day in 1998, the club chairman, Fintan Murtagh, came over to me in the Blackthorn: 'We need your help badly if we're to go anywhere in this championship.' I agreed to help. I put a lot of work into promoting the club, and invested a few bob to enable them to bring over a few players from Ireland. I brought over Pat Roe, who was one of the best players that I've ever seen playing in Boston – and I've seen many of them. Pat managed the Wexford senior footballers to the Leinster semifinal this year. I also brought over Scott Doran from Wexford and Wayne Daly, who had a couple of championship games under his belt with the Dubs. We put together a great run in the championship and made it to the final, where we were trailing by a point with a minute to go.

'*Déja vu*, here we go again,' I muttered to myself, as memories of times past with Tyrrellspass, St Pat's and Wolfe Tones flashed before my eyes. But I always had great faith in Wayne. In the dying moments, he won the ball in the centre of the field and kicked it into Scott, who fired to the net to ensure we won the game by two points.

When Brendan and myself started up the team, I had promised that, if Wolfe Tones ever won the championship, I'd get down on the ground and kiss South Boston Bridge. That day, I was reminded of my promise! When we were coming home on the Sunday evening with the cup, we stopped all the traffic. I had to get out and kneel on the ground and kiss the bridge. It was a fantastic feeling to see the club that I was so deeply involved with winning the intermediate championship.

While the celebrations were in full swing in the Blackthorn, I got up on the bar to make a speech with Wayne beside me. He accidentally pushed me and sent me flying off the bar. I hit my rib cage off the side of a beer cooler and broke a few ribs. 'Get an ambulance, get an ambulance,' shouted somebody. 'Don't call no f***in' ambulance to this pub, get me up and get me out of here,' was all I could say.

I wasn't able to get out of the bed the next day, and three or four of the lads had to come down and bring me up to hospital. I missed all the celebrations that week. I was determined to get myself right, because Wolfe Tones had qualified for the All American championships down in San Francisco. I went to San Francisco armed with plenty of painkillers. We made it to the final, where the hosts defeated us. I ended up in hospital in San Francisco, because my broken ribs were lying against my lung. An Irish-American doctor eventually sorted me out and I got on a plane back to Boston.

The Wolfe Tones club was close to my heart, but when we opened the Boston Baggot, I was asked whether we would we sponsor the McAnespies club, another senior team in Boston. I decided to keep sponsoring the Wolfe Tones in the Blackthorn, while going ahead and sponsoring the McAnespies with the Baggot. However, some of the Tones' lads took exception to me sponsoring the McAnespies and pulled a coup against me. At this stage, the Blackthorn and Shenanigans, a restaurant-bar, were co-sponsoring the Wolfe Tones.

In 2000, the club's AGM was held in one of the lad's apartments. The Shenanigans crew said that they were going to sponsor the Wolfe Tones on their own. 'Sure, I'll do the same if that's the way it's going to be,' I replied. 'I'll put up the same amount of money and I'll sponsor them fully.' But I knew the coup had been worked out beforehand. Then they wanted to soften me up and put me in as vice-chairman. I felt at this stage that my time was up with the Wolfe Tones, but I remain great friends with all the lads. For the next couple of years that I remained in the Boston Baggot, I sponsored the McAnespies and Father Tom's hurling club.

The Blackthorn was often a calling point for visiting Gaelic teams from Ireland. Indeed, one of the best weeks we ever had in the place was during the early 1990s when the Glen Rovers camogie squad arrived in Boston for a few games. Or maybe I should say they arrived in the Blackthorn! The Rebel women had just been beaten in the All Ireland final, so they took a break to drown their sorrows. As luck would have it, Cork's finest stout, Murphy's, was being connected up in the bar on the day that the women arrived in. Mary Ring, daughter of the great hurler, Christy Ring, was belting out Christy Moore songs. I asked the girls whether they liked Murphy's and the reply that came back across the bar was: 'Does a cat like milk, Frankie?'

Captain Linda Mellerick and her crew forced the Murphy's rep to give them a free keg of stout. It was the quickest barrel of

Murphy's that was ever drank in the Blackthorn. It didn't do them any harm, though. A couple of years later, I was privileged to be with the Cork team when they won the 1995 All Ireland at Croke Park. I filled the O'Duffy Cup in Big Jack's Baggot Inn in Dublin later that week.

In 1995, the Westmeath minor footballers lifted the All Ireland title for the first time, defeating Derry in Croke Park – a match I missed due to a dreadful bout of 'flu. After that momentous breakthrough by Luke Dempsey's side, everybody in the county held its breath hoping that the seniors would be able to build on this win. Football fans with a real knowledge of the game knew it would take some time, and the under-21's superb All Ireland final win in 1999 confirmed this.

Many of us felt that the train had left the station for the Westmeath senior side in the first few years of the new millennium. Westmeath was one of the three remaining football counties which had never won a provincial crown. That was made worse by the fact that the team lost Leinster championship matches which they should have won against old rivals Meath. So, when legendary former Kerry footballer and county manager Páidí Ó Sé was appointed the new senior county coach in November 2003, we thought that God himself had descended into the county. Here was the man who would finally deliver the Holy Grail of a Leinster title.

I first met Páidí many years ago in Boston, and he has been a great friend ever since. One night, I was in Páidí's famous pub in Ventry, where he told me a few stories about the great Kerry–Dublin games of the 1970s. One night at training, a few of the new lads on the Kerry team were plotting how to get in and give the great Dublin goalie Paddy Cullen 'a slap'. 'I was listening discreetly,' said Páidí, 'but saying nothing, when someone asked what I thought of the idea to give Cullen a dig. "Jaysus, lads, ye'll have no problem getting in, but did yiz ever think how yiz might get out!" I told them.'

Páidí won more All Ireland senior football medals than he could hold in one hand. On top of his eight Sam Maguire successes as a player, he had led Kerry to two of the last seven Sam Maguire titles as manager. I couldn't believe my ears when I heard Páidí was taking the Westmeath job. I was so delighted that I made the trip home to be at his first press conference in Mullingar, bringing with me a card wishing him good luck from all the Westmeath supporters in Boston.

As usual I got a great welcome from Páidí, and that night he invited me to Dublin where he was appearing on the Eamonn Dunphy show on TV3. We were picked up at his hotel in Dublin by a taxi and driven to the Helix Theatre out in DCU for the show. The taxi driver turned to Páidí and said 'Jesus, Páidí, ya have your work cut out with them shower of f***ers down in Westmeath. Are ya all right in the head or wha'?' Páidí laughed, clapped the taxi driver's back and replied: 'My dear man, Páidí Ó Sé made the Dubs walk off a short plank before and I might just do it again.' Páidí's words must be still haunting our taxi driver!

The enthusiasm that greeted Páidí's appointment to the Westmeath job was reflected by the crowds who turned up in Cusack Park for the team's National Football League games in the New Year. Some 14,000 crammed in to watch the O'Byrne Cup final against Meath and the excitement was on a par with the near-hysteria that I had witnessed in Irish supporters at World Cup finals.

No longer was the Westmeath football team regarded as simply making up the numbers. Páidí was in charge and the talented squad was now on a mission. However, a few defeats soon saw the fair-weather fans drift away, and the start of some carping over Páidí's ability to deliver the goods. The maestro soon shut the Doubting Thomases up: on 13 May, 2004, we beat our ancient rivals Offaly by 0–11 to 0–10 in the first round of the Leinster

PÁIDÍ DELIVERS THE HOLY GRAIL

championship – our first win over them since 1949. The win was secured without the services of Westmeath's All-Star midfielder, Rory O'Connell, who was sent off by referee Pat Russell during the match.

Watching my Tyrrellspass neighbour Dennis Glennon playing so well at full forward, alongside the outstanding Dessie Dolan, made my heart pound that bit quicker. I thought it was going to burst when Michael Ennis fisted over the winning point. Feck the league, it's the championship that counts and Páidí knows it!

With that famous victory secured, it was on to Croke Park to face the Dubs on 6 June. Very few people gave us a chance of stopping the Dubs from booking their semifinal place. Because of the draw, they were going into the match without a championship outing under their belts. History fancied Tommy Lyons' men, whom we had not beaten since 1967. We won by 0–14 to 0–12 with a display of football that left the Dubs dumbfounded. Until the day I die, I'll treasure the moment when the referee's final whistle sounded. Could it be true? Were we one game away from the Leinster final?

Standing between us and that final was my old Wolfe Tones' club mate, Pat Roe, and his Wexford team. With the amazing scoring machine Mattie Forde in their ranks, this Wexford team was not to be lightly dismissed. Our win over Dublin made us most people's favourites even though Wexford had shocked Kildare in their quarter-final tie. I was really nervous as we made our way to the banks of the Royal Canal on 27 June because losing would have been unthinkable. But I need not have worried, as we triumphed by 2–15 to 1–14 in an absorbing tussle that saw the brilliant Dessie Dolan clock up 1–7. Westmeath were now set for their first appearance in a Leinster senior football final since 1949.

Now for the provincial showdown against Mick O'Dwyer's Laois, who had surprised everybody in the country 12 months earlier by lifting the county's first Leinster crown in 57 years. The master Micko now faced his former cunning pupil Páidí, and the entire world of Gaelic football was enthralled. Páidí had played under the great Kerry manager Micko during the 1970s and 1980s.

Thankfully, Westmeath had been restored to its usual status as underdog. Off we trooped to Croke Park on Sunday, 18 July. You could almost see Páidí licking his lips in anticipation as Pat McEnaney threw in the ball to signal the start of the game. This was Denis Glennon's day in the sun, as he attacked the Laois backs at will. He ended the match with 0–5, as Westmeath did enough to win the title. But our hearts were broken three minutes into injury time, when Chris Conway calmly kicked the equalising point to leave the teams level at 0–13 each. It would mean a return trip to Dublin the following Saturday. Westmeath had to do without my support in the replay as I flew back to Boston two days later with Melanie. I seriously considered staying in Ireland but there was business to attend to back in the States.

On Saturday morning, I headed down to the Banshee pub in Boston with dozens of other Westmeath and Laois supporters to watch the final act of this nerve-racking final on TV. With me were Donna, Trevor, Melanie, the Murtagh family, Finbar Coyne, Mike Carey and Brian McCabe. Despite warnings from all quarters that Laois would win the day, it was the men in maroon and white who triumphed by 0–12 to 0–10. I sang, I danced, I shouted, I cried with joy, I hugged complete strangers, I phoned as many people I could think of, I texted many more and I drank my fill that day and night. I wasn't physically in Croke Park or Tyrrellspass but my spirit was in both places.

Páidí had inspired a relatively young team into believing that they could win the Leinster title. We were the best team in the province and now we had to beat Derry to reach the last four in Ireland. On Sunday, 18 August, I again trekked to the Banshee to take my ringside seat. Derry had reached this point through the backdoor route, after suffering an 11-point mauling by their great rivals Tyrone in the first round of the Ulster championship. But were now up and running under the shrewd Mickey Moran.

Maybe it was the exertions of the previous games – particularly the replay win over Laois – but the Westmeath lads never found their true rhythm that afternoon. We more than matched Derry when it came to scoring points, but the goals by Paddy Bradley and Enda Muldoon gave Derry a 2–5 to 0–7 halftime lead. They held on until the final whistle, winning by 2–9 to 0–13.

Our disappointment ran deep, but we had to salute the players, Páidí and his selectors for what they had achieved this year. Westmeath football grew up, and we showed that we can mix with and beat the best. It also leaves me with a hearty desire to finally bring Sam back to this part of the midlands. And when that happens, I've already told Páidí that first stop when it crosses the Atlantic is the Blackthorn bar in South Boston.

Thanks to the following people:

To the people of America, especially Boston, for giving me and my family a good life. To Brendan Lenehan for making the call and bringing me to Boston. To Christine O'Brien for picking me up at the airport, helping me and giving me so much encouragement in the early stages of this book. To Mike O'Connor, Chris Sullivan, Pat Bligh and St Patrick's Gaelic football club. To Chris Barrett for my first job. To the Bullman family for looking after me and my family and giving us so much love and attention.

To Joe McGlone for my first $1,000 loan and to Tom and Cathy Mitchell of Cunningham Electric. To the Irish community in Boston for all their great support over the past 14 years in the Blackthorn. To all the staff over the years in the Blackthorn, the DJs Dan Hallisey, Colm O'Brien and Macca. To the numerous bands, especially the Altar Boys, Paul Duffy, the Millionaires, Patsy and Pat, Christy O'Connell, Brendan Grace, Brendan O'Carroll, Bagatelle, Paddy Reilly, the Barleycorn (not forgetting my late friend Derek McCormack who died this year), the Dublin City Ramblers, my adopted brothers the Fureys, the Wolfe Tones, the Chieftains and Michael Flatley for all his kindness.

To the Irish in New York, San Francisco and Chicago for always extending a warm 'Céad Míle Fáilte', especially PJ and Tom Quinn. To Willie Lowry, Dessie Costello from the Westmeath team in New York, Rory Dolan, Mike Carthy, Tom Nolan, Rosie O'Grady's, McSorley's and Barry McCormack's Bar. To Fitzpatrick's Hotels, PJ Carney's, Paddy McCarthy (formerly of *The Irish Voice*), Niall O'Dowd of *The Irish Voice*.

To all my fellow publicans in Boston, especially my local Nash's. To Eileen Fox, Mike Gargan and Jack. To Shenanigans, the Lir, McGanns, the Littlest Bar, the Irish Embassy Bar, Mr Dooley's, Tiernan's, the Times, Róisín Dubh, the Junction, the Banshee Beer Garden, the Playwright, the Erie Pub, Paddy Barry's, Bad Abbott's, Sarsfields, Peddlers and the Daughter in Haverhill.

To Martin Connelly, Foley's in San Francisco, Mick O'Brien, Father Brendan McBride, Shane and Robert from Setanta and all my publican friends in San Fran – too numerous to name. My dear friend Father Ted Linehan for all the great work you did for the Irish community in Boston and also our pal Mick Harhen and all my friends and neighbours in Quincy.

To all the people of Tyrrellspass. Thanks for a great childhood, the oodles of fond memories and for the great welcome home I get each time I'm there. To Mick McGuire, his wife, Phil, and family for giving me a bed and great food. To Jody Gonoud, Willie in the Esker and the Spinning Wheel for good porter. To 'the Boiler' for my petrol on tick and to Johnny's hardware for all the credit. To the Byrne family for all their courtesy and kindness in their shop and post office.

To Tom Fitzpatrick and all the girls in your shop, to the Tidy Towns Committee for the great work you do in the village. To the drama class for staging great plays every year. To Dr Clyne for the prescriptions and Mark for the drugs (the right sort). To the Castle and Hotel for great steaks.

To Tyrrellspass GAA club for great pleasure in the past and present. Thanks for the Colonel's guard of honour at his funeral. To Páidí Ó Sé and Thomas O'Flatharta, the senior county team selectors, the Westmeath supporters club and my neighbour Tommy Glennon for all their brilliant work with the Westmeath team.

To my Auntie Kate for helping to rear me. To Larry Arthur for all the jobs. The late Mrs Kelly, our midwife, who helped bring us all into this world. To the retirement home for your great work with the elderly. To all the staff at St Mary's hospital in Mullingar. To all the doctors, nurses and medical staff for their care and attention given to Melanie and myself after our horrific accident and also to the firemen of Mullingar for getting Melanie free from the car.

To all my many friends in Dublin – Fran Ryder, Larry Shane, Murph, Alex and Jack Sheedy in the Mill. To the Mercantile, the Submarine, Muldowney's Rathcoole, the Red Cow, Mrs Lee's in Ringwood, the Thatch in Newcastle (I miss it, please rebuild it, Paul and Aisling!). To Chris Byrne and family for your great friendship and for letting me be your buddy. To Aer Lingus, especially Pauline Vaughan, John Lawlor, Brendan Singleton-Warren, Keith Lancaster (happy retirement) and all the staff in Boston, Shannon and Dublin for many years of safe travelling.

To Anglo Irish, Dan O'Driscoll of AIB, Declan McKiernan, Dave McKenna and family for the trips to Old Trafford. To all my friends on Baggot Street, Gerry and Ann for the flowers. To Toners, O'Donoghues, Doheny and Nesbitts. To the late Gerry Drew for many's a good laugh. To all the people I have written about in this book, thank you all for your great friendship and love.

To Kathleen Poynton for all the great advice and care. To Mike Foley – a great manager of the Blackthorn – and his family, and good luck in Nancy Whiskeys in Carlow. To my dear friend Big Jack Charlton, for his great work in changing the course of Ireland's soccer history, for his kindness to me and my family, for helping me catch my first salmon, for our great venture in business and for taking the time to launch this book. I love you, ya big lank. To his wife Pat, sons John and Peter, daughter Debbie and family and John's girlfriend, Deirdre.

To Cathal Dervan for giving me the idea to write this book many years ago. To the Irish players who took me under their wings and gave me great excitement all over the world. To Kevin Moran – you are always there for advice, a ticket, a chat or just a pint. And to your lovely wife Eleanor and family and all the Morans in Dublin. To Mick and Breda Byrne and their family. Mick, you were a father and mother to us all; you always gave me a bed and a warm welcome.

To Aldo, you will always be a great pal, to your wife, Joan, son Paul and daughter Joanne. To Stan – you're the man who has always looked after me. To Paul McGrath, a legend and a good friend – thanks for all the great bedtime stories in the Nuremore Hotel.

To Ronnie Whelan – I saved your bacon in Florida with a good left hook. To Packie Bonner for the great sing songs, especially your rendition of 'The Homes of Donegal'. To Denis Irwin – I will always remember the Chester Races in 1993. To Niall and Gillian Quinn who always had a bed for me. To Niall's dad, Billy, a true Tip man, with whom I always enjoy a pint or backing a winner. You sang for the Colonel – thanks a million.

To Alan Kelly, a gentle giant; Gary Kelly always a giver; Andy Townsend, a great leader; to Andy's brother and my ex-roommate, Mike; to Jason McAteer and Phil Babb – it was always a pleasure to have you on holiday in Boston. To Tony Cascarino, our 'Ice Cream Man' whose jokes are still in my head. To Mick McCarthy, you gave my son Trevor your full Irish playing kit. To Tommy Coyne, a really strong man. To Ray Houghton – I minded your son during that great game in Giants stadium and you returned the favour by scoring a great goal and buying my son his first pint. To Terry Phelan, you ran like a greyhound. To Alan McLoughlin, thanks for all the match tickets and for the goal that brought us to the World Cup in 1994. To Mossie and Marie Keane and family for always giving me a fantastic 'Céad Míle Fáilte'. To Roy Keane for his friendship and the craic in the Templeacre.

To my publisher Blackwater Press and company MD John O'Connor for having the courage and the faith in me to publish this book. To Margaret Burns and Ciara McNee of Blackwater for all their help in realising the project.

To my great pal Sean 'Spud' Murphy – everyone should have friends like you and your wife, Barbara. To Peter for driving me to Kinnegad with my mobile. To Eileen Grace for always being a great host, to your mum Lily, the O'Connor, Farrell and McShera families.

To Larry Mullen of U2 for taking care of me, for the tickets to the concerts and most of all making me feel very welcome. To Ann for the cigs in LA and for your visits to the Blackthorn and Baggot. To Joe O'Herlihy and his wife Marian and family. To John Mallen for work in tough times and his financial support for this book. To Mick and Mary Carley for many years of chats and fun.

To the Glennons, Ryans, Daltons and Pauline and Paddy O'Brien. To Peter Fagan and family for being so good to Alice. To the Connors of Meedin and Newbridge, to Barney and all the Morgans. To the Dunnes, Duffys, McCormacks, Downes, O'Briens, Forans of Dublin and Mullallys in Tallaght.

To Joe McCadden, Kevin Macken in Celtic Real Estate in Florida. To all my friends in Jupiter, Florida, especially in Rooney's, McCarthy's and O'Shea's bars. To my godmother Betty Mooney and godfather, the late Vincent Mooney. To the McGees, especially Hubert, for all your visits to the Colonel.

To my dearest girlfriend Melanie for your great support and patience and for also composing the poem on the book launch invitations. Who love's ya baby! To Donna and Trevor for your love that keeps me smiling. To all my family and friends in Tyrrellspass and around the world and to the people that I did not get to mention because space constraints – there is space in my heart, thank you too.